Equals

Equals

ADAM PHILLIPS

BASIC
BOOKS

A Member of the Perseus Books Group

A cataloging-in-publication record for this book is available from the
Library of Congress.
ISBN 0-465-05679-2
02 03 04 / 10 9 8 7 6 5 4 3 2 1

for Frank Kermode and Christopher Bollas

The necessity of speaking of dancers with
exclamation marks.
Kafka, *Diaries 1912*

So many versions at any time are all exemplary...
Douglas Crase, 'The Lake Effect'

The truth lies not in one of the disputed views
but in some third possibility which has not yet been
thought of, which we can only discover by
rejecting something assumed as obvious
by both the disputants.
F. P. Ramsey, 'Universals'

Circumlocution is another matter.
Donald Davie, *Purity of Diction in English Verse*

Contents

ACKNOWLEDGEMENTS

Several of the pieces in this book were first published, some in different versions, in *London Review of Books*, *Raritan*, *Index*, *New Formations* and *Threepenny Review*. I am grateful, as ever, to the editors of these journals.

'The Soul of Man under Psychoanalysis' was given as the T. S. Eliot Memorial Lecture in 2001 at the University of Kent at Canterbury. 'Making It Old' was given as a lecture at the Tate Britain conference 'The Presence of the Past' in 2001.

Preface

If the best thing we do is look after each other, then the worst thing we do is pretend to look after each other when in fact we are doing something else. One of the many disturbing things about psychoanalysis – as a description of who we are, and as a kind of help – is that it shows us why it is often so difficult to tell these things apart. Or rather, it shows us that this distinction, upon which most of our morality depends, is often spurious because we are always likely to be doing both things at once (and several more). Love is not enough, because love is fraught with hatred. It is to what is being taken when we take care of another person that Freud drew our attention.

At our most rationally optimistic we can acknowledge the starker ambiguities of the simplest exchange, and just think of it as a question of proportion, of getting our (emotional) sums right; of there being more love than hate in the equation, enough good will despite the other kinds of will. But once we stop trying to measure feelings – stop describing our feelings as like things that can be quantified – the new morality of helping people that is ushered in by psychoanalysis seems rather more complicated. If we are, as psychoanalysis proposes, the ambivalent animals, then doing good is a form of doing harm, and vice versa; purity of heart vanishes as an ideal, and niceness begins to look rather more interesting than it seemed. 'We would not be surprised', the psychoanalyst Harold Searles writes, to find that a surgeon brings forth, in the course of his psycho-analysis, powerful and heretofore deeply repressed wishes physic-ally to dismember other people, so we should be ready to discern the presence, in not a few of us who have chosen the profession of treating psychiatric illness, of similarly powerful, long-repressed desires to dismember the personality structure of other persons.

That we can help each other is self-evident (who else can help us if we can't?). What psychoanalysis suggests is that the whole notion of helping people is one of our favourite cover-stories for the moral complexity of exchange.

It is always too easy – as philanthropy has never been able to hide – for us to live as though we know what it is to help another person. And this is partly because it involves knowing – or assuming we know, as we often have to do with children – what is good for them, whether or not it is their chosen good. Psychoanalysis proposes that we are unconscious of the good we seek; and that to simply (and solely) call it good is something of a misnomer. Clearly we can only help people if we have some notion of what is good for them; and so we need ways – of which psychoanalysis is one – of finding out from them just what this might be (and, of course, we need to believe that it is good for us to find out what is good for them; and this belief, one could say, is part of the democratic impulse). This book is about, among various other things, what the phrase 'the chosen good' – and, indeed, the idea of knowing what is good for someone – might mean after the inventions of psychoanalysis.

Calling psychoanalysis a talking cure has obscured the sense in which it is a listening cure (and the senses in which it is not a cure at all). Being listened to can enable one to bear – and even to enjoy – listening to oneself and others; which democracy itself depends upon. Whether or not the whole notion of equality was invented to make it possible for people to listen to each other, or vice versa, listening is privileged in democratic societies. As an education in forms of attention – as, that is to say, essentially a democratic art – psychoanalysis reveals what two people (at least) can feel and think and say in each other's presence if they don't have sex with each other. It is an experiment, like democracy, in what people can bear about each other, in what they are equal to. When Nietzsche wrote, in *Beyond Good and Evil*, ' "I do not like it." – Why? – "I am not up to it." Has anyone ever answered like that?', he was alluding to this very common sense of somehow not being equal to something; and how our morality (and our other aesthetic judgements) can be a self-cure for precisely this experience. What it might be to look after someone now, and the someone who is oneself, involves imagining – as theories of psychoanalysis and theories of democracy both intimate – what, at any given moment, we (and they) are equal to.

That people are not identical, but that it is possible for them to be equal in certain ways, is one of our modern political hopes. Despite the vivid inequalities of wealth, prestige, history, talent and beauty there are certain cultural goods that can be shared by everybody. For this to be plausible and not merely inspiring we have to have descriptions of just where, or in what, this elusive equality resides (other, that is, than in our consenting to not give up on the idea of equality). The psychoanalytic opportunity – the nature and arrangement of psychoanalytic treatment – is, I want to suggest in this book, an unusually ideal setting in which to explore these issues.

One cannot, in all honesty, say, 'I'll tell you a great joke'; one can only say, 'I'll tell you a joke.' The decision is always in the one who listens, not in the one who speaks. This is the model.

EQUALS

Superiorities

... stability does not depend on the immutability of individual particles but solely on the dynamics of their interaction.

Evelyn Fox Keller, *The Century of the Gene*

In 1945, just after the end of the war, Lacan came to London as a French psychiatrist to find out about the effect of the war on British psychiatry. His report on his visit, *British Psychiatry and the War*, was published early in 1947. What Lacan is evidently most impressed by is his meeting with Bion and Rickman, and their accounts of their work in small groups with soldiers who, for various reasons, were debilitated and needed some kind of help. There are, as one might expect given the historical moment and the personalities involved, many fascinating things in Lacan's impressions and celebrations of this early psychoanalytic work with groups that has turned out to be so influential. But there is a thread running through Lacan's paper, a preoccupation that punctuates whatever else he is saying, that is clearly linked with his first official contribution to the psychoanalytic group on the mirror stage. What Lacan keeps returning to – perhaps unsurprisingly after the devastations of the war against fascism – is the idea, the modern political ideal, of equality. In the mirror-stage paper

3

Lacan shows how we are never equal to our (unified) image of ourselves; that what the child sees in the mirror is, as it were, his complementary rival. If Freud had proposed in his structural theory of the mind that there was not, and could never be, internal equality between his various 'agencies', Lacan had added to this unending uncivil war an image of the child diminished, tyrannised and enraged by his wished-for self-representation. Whether or not Freud or Lacan (at this time) thought of themselves as democrats, or believed in equality as one of the rights of man, there is nothing in their psychoanalytic accounts of what people are really like that is conducive to the kind of social hope invested in ideas of equality. Indeed one might think, from a psychoanalytic point of view, that equality – like many of the other so-called rights of man – was ripe for ironisation. Something, perhaps, along the lines of Joan Riviere's infamous, and possibly apocryphal remark that socialism was the religion of younger siblings.

And yet in Lacan's paper – even in its tone of idealistic pessimism generated by the experience of the war – it is as though he cannot give up on something about the notion of equality. Despite Freud's work on group psychology, despite the daunting, invasive subtleties of forms of identification; despite the fact that, as he puts it, 'the dark powers of the super-ego make alliances with the most cowardly abandonments of conscience', he is interested in this paper in what might be called alternatives to leadership. If his early work on the family was about the consequences of the modern destitution of what he called the 'paternal imago', it is to redescriptions of the notion of leadership – of what we might call, sociologically, the problem not only of authority but of the fantasy of the authoritative – that he is drawn through his encounter with the British. In Bion's work, Lacan writes, the analyst, as group leader, 'will undertake to organise the situation so as to force the group to become aware of the difficulties of its existence as a group, and then render it more and more transparent to itself, to the point where each of its members may be able to judge adequately the progress of the whole'. As Lacan puts it, this is a version, to use his word, of forcing people to become equals. Clearly the aim of arriving at a point 'where each of its members may be able to judge adequately the progress of the whole', is to arrive at the point at which the position of leader disappears. It is a description of what one might want to be going on, ideally, in a certain kind of democracy. But of course it has to be noted, firstly, that it requires a group leader to get the members of the group to this point, through his psychoanalytic method. And secondly there is, and will always be, the question of who decides what it is to 'judge adequately the progress of the group'. Where, one can ask, do the criteria for adequate judgement come from? What has the group consented to when it acknowledges any judgement as adequate, or even unusually valuable? When what Lacan refers to as 'the crystallisation of an autocritique materialising in the group' occurs, it is as though the psychoanalytic method of enquiry has given each and all the members of the group a shared, and therefore consented to, genre of useful judgement. They enjoy a new sense of know-how in common. But what is this autocritique like? It could, for example, be like the group having agreed to the rules of a game; but agreeing to the rules of a game doesn't stop some people being better at it than others. Indeed, one could say it creates the conditions under which people can distinguish themselves. It is only because there are rules that have been consented to, that prestige, that inequalities begin to emerge. To consent to a

5

set of rules is to set up a potential hierarchy. By putting a basic structure of equality in place, by providing a base-line of sameness, differences can come through. The question lurking here – which seems like a question tailor-made for psychoanalysis – is: Why is hierarchy the reflex response to difference? But Lacan intimates here that, at least in his description of the Bion group, the psychoanalytic method can make possible the enjoyment, the productive use of difference. If everyone gets to the point of being able to 'judge adequately the progress of the group' they must have some shared sense, however tacit, of what constitutes progress; of what it is better for the group to be doing. And yet, of course, we know that too much consensus, just like too little, is the enemy of democracy.

It is when Lacan refers in his paper to a comment made by Rickman that he begins to form, if not quite to formulate, his question. Rickman, he says, 'makes the following remark, which to some will seem striking, that if one can say that the neurotic is ego-centric and loathes any effort of co-operation, it is perhaps because he is rarely placed in an environment where every member would be on the same footing as himself when it comes to relating to one's counterpart'. One's immediate response to this striking remark is, where could there be such an environment? Because this, surely, is an environment of absolute equality. And yet to behave as if one is on the same footing with others – or on the same footing with regard to certain conditions – is a virtual definition of equality, if not of democracy. What would it be, for example, what would psychoanalytic treatment, which Lacan preferred to call psychoanalytic experience, be like, if the analyst considered himself to be on the same footing as the so-called patient? It is the need for superiority, the need to be the exception, the

6

need to exempt oneself from something that Rickman is using the word neurotic to describe. As though a neurotic was someone who needed to believe that he had a distinguishing feature, that there was something special about him (and this might lead us to wonder how free we might feel if we were nothing special). Lacan refers later in his paper to what he calls, with a certain necessary archness, the 'noli me tangere that one finds more than frequently at the root of the medical vocation no less than that in the man of God and the man of Law. Indeed these are the three professions which assure a man that he will find himself in a position in which superiority over his interlocutor is guaranteed in advance.' Of course Lacan's omission of the analyst – of psychoanalysis as the fourth profession that is a bit like each of the three he mentions – is essential here. In psychoanalysis there is no touching and it is, as it were, the redemptive wishes that are to be analysed.

And yet here we have, in a paper that is nothing if not celebratory of what Lacan calls the 'revolution' created by psychoanalysis, the juxtaposition of two images, of two insinuating descriptions. We have Rickman's neurotic, ego-centric and loathing of co-operation, because he is rarely placed or indeed places himself 'in an environment where every member would be on the same footing as himself when it comes to relating to one's counter-part'; and we have the doctors, the lawyers and the men of God, 'professions which assure a man that he will find himself in a position in which superiority over his interlocutor is guaranteed in advance'. The neurotics, like these great and legitimate professionals, need to exclude themselves from something, need to reject something in advance. They must, in one way or another, be untouchable. It is, to exaggerate, as if their lives depended upon their not having equals. It is

7

some notion of equality that they are phobic of. So what could it be about equality – what does equality entail, or involve us in – that could make it so aversive? To be treated by one's interlocutor as superior or different in advance places one's interlocutor in a threatening position; as though what could be lost in losing one's superiority, one's prestige, however variously defined, is deemed to be catastrophic. The analyst, Lacan will later famously say, is the one who is supposed to know; the person, perhaps, in whom the patient delegates his superiority. And among the targets of Lacan's later critique of the psychoanalytic establishment will be those psychoanalytic institutions and theorists who put themselves in a position in which their superiority over their interlocutors is guaranteed in advance. In other words, for Lacan psychoanalysis is about the way the individual suffers – and loves to suffer – his terror of equality. Psychoanalysis addresses how an individual excludes himself, exempts himself, distances himself from certain kinds of association. As though the modern, the 'civilised' form of what anthropologists called participation mystique is a horror of participation mystique.

There is something about equality, something about the absence of superiority guaranteed in advance, that psycho-analysis has something to say about. And it is not merely one's own superiority; it may simply be the need to believe that there are some people – and that we can have some kind of connection with them – whose superiority is guaranteed in advance. It could be a deity or a celebrity, it could be a race or a nation-state; it could even be a psychoanalytic training institute. But without this superiority existing somewhere in a person's orbit, they – we – are destitute. Clearly, it is not incompatible to be committed to democracy and to dread equality – and so, in the name of democracy, to foster forms of prestige. The forbidden thought may be that there is more pleasure in being less special; that self-importance is the enemy of self-satisfaction.

There are two questions here: what would equality feel like such that people might organise their lives to avoid it? And does psychoanalysis, as Lacan intimates in this early paper – and the trials and tribulations of his life's work bear witness to the demanding perplexities of this – have anything akin to a cure for the wish for a superiority guaranteed in advance? Or to put it rather differently, has psychoanalysis got anything to do with democracy?

II

The fact that the presence of deliberately introduced extraneous stimuli frequently improves performance has been regarded as a curious paradox ...

Harry Scott, quoted in *Harry's Absence* by Jonathan Scott

'When we envisage democratic politics from ... an anti-essentialist perspective,' Chantal Mouffe writes in *The Democratic Paradox*, 'we can begin to understand that for democracy to exist, no social agent should be able to claim any mastery of the foundation of society.' They would be unable to claim it because from this point of view there is no foundation of society available to be mastered. Indeed, one could say that it is the existence of foundations – or rather, the fantasy of their existence – that itself makes mastery possible. No one in a democracy, in Mouffe's account, has a superiority guaranteed in advance, at least when they are acting democratically. Would it not, after all, be constitutive – would it not be a virtual definition – of Lacan's notion of the superiority of the medical profession, the judiciary and the church that each of these professions claim some kind of mastery of the foundations of their own society, if not of every society? The kind of equalities implied by democracy – what each person in a democracy relatively freely consents to – has to set new kinds of limits to mastery. Democracy, as Mouffe describes it, involves redescribing the whole notion of leadership, and the value of conflict.

Defining antagonism as the struggle between enemies, and agonism as the struggle between adversaries, Mouffe proposes what she calls 'agonistic pluralism'. 'The aim of democratic politics', she writes,

is to transform antagonism into agonism ... One of the keys to the thesis of agonistic puralism is that, far from jeopardising democracy, agonistic confrontation is in fact its very condition of existence. Modern democracy's specificity lies in the recognition and legitimation of conflict and the refusal to suppress it by imposing an authoritarian order ... a democratic society acknowledges the pluralism of values.

From a psychoanalytic point of view, Mouffe's version of democratic politics is an interesting provocation. We are more likely, for example, to feel superior to our enemies than to our adversaries. Indeed the whole idea of an enemy makes the idea of superiority possible, if not plausible (it may not be enemies we are in pursuit of, but states of inner superiority). If we use Mouffe's picture as what used to be called a model of the mind – and what I would prefer to call a conjecture about what people are really like – and if we map her model of democracy back on to what some psychoanalysts call the internal world, we will at first find a great deal of reassurance. Isn't it, after all, one of the aims of at least some versions of psychoanalysis to transform enemies into adversaries; to free a person to be at odds with himself (and others) rather than in lethal combat. If agonistic

confrontation is the very condition of democracy's existence, can we not say that by the same token, conflict is the
individual's life-support system? And yet, of course,
psychoanalytic schools can be defined by the internal and
external points of view they are prepared to credit. What,
for example, would be an internal pluralism of values?
Could the racism of the self find a voice here, and what kind
of voice would that be? What is perhaps most interesting in
Mouffe's formulation is the definition of the authoritarian as
that which suppresses conflict. As though it is the very
existence of conflict itself that certain versions of authority
cannot bear. And this might be a clue to what is intolerable
about equality. What the person whose superiority is
guaranteed in advance cannot bear is the protracted
sustaining, indeed existence of conflict. Equality then is
the legitimation, if not the celebration, of conflict. Is it then
possible, from a psychoanalytic point of view, to think of a
person as – or to free a person to be – internally adversarial?
That is, more of a democrat through and through? It could
legitimately be said that people come for psychoanalysis,
people suffer, because they have suppressed a conflict by
imposing an authoritarian order. They feel coerced, and
they are coercive (the coerciveness is called symptoms by
the so-called patient and transference by the so-called
analyst). People experience and describe themselves as
living under various forms of domination and oppression.
The analysis discloses an unconscious authoritarian order
called the super-ego. And it is indeed illuminating to think
of the super-ego not as the cause of conflict but as the
saboteur of conflict.

And yet, if we take up Lacan's evident privileging of
psychoanalysis as being somehow part of a project to free
the individual – without exaggerating or idealising the

kinds of freedom that may be on offer – as having found, through the experience of war, defining opportunities and occasions to think about the direction, the project of psychoanalysis; both what it might have to offer and what it might want to offer; that is, to consider the values it promoted; then we have to think carefully about psycho-analysis in the light of Chantal Mouffe's sentence. 'Modern democracy's specificity lies in the recognition and legitima-tion of conflict and the refusal to suppress it by imposing an authoritarian order.' The authoritarian order pre-empts conflict, which is in and of itself a primary value. And to value conflict – to prefer the openness of conflict to the closure of intimidation – necessitates some notion of equality. Conflict that is not between equals ceases to be conflict very quickly. It becomes the simulacrum of conflict called sado-masochism. We may wonder what the pre-conditions are, both psychicly and politically, for keeping conflict alive and viable. And in wondering that we might wonder both what a democratic psychoanalysis would be like; and what, to put it as modestly as possible, psycho-analysis may have to offer, if anything, to the making of democrats (better and better descriptions of the nature and value of conflict could be one candidate). Whether its practice – its writings, its trainings, the set-up of its clinical work – persuades people to identify with democratic values. It would be good, for example, if as Laplanche says a transference is never resolved, only displaced; that the outcome of a successful analysis would be that a person would be able to bear to listen to what other people have to say. That through the experience of analysis a person might rediscover an appetite for talking and for listening and for disagreement. Which is an appetite for democracy.

The subject who is supposed to know turns into the

person with a passion for listening; for the after-effects of listening. Speaking becomes worth doing because it is conducive of conflict. But conflict is not a version of pastoral. The equality in Mouffe's version of democracy, such as it is, could never be an equality of wealth, or talent, or beauty. The only equality that exists in it is in each person an equality of rivenness, an equality of unknowingness, the equality born of there being no foundations to master. In a mix of languages we might say that the will is displaced by the idea of the unconscious: and mastery is displaced by temporary forms of consensus. We do not know what we are doing but we have things that we must do. We are, like all creatures, creatures who want; and yet, for some reason we are unable to dispense with the idea of justice (even the immoral seem obliged to give moral justifications for their actions). So what then would a psychoanalysis be like, in practice, that recognised and legitimated conflict, and refused to suppress it by imposing an authoritarian order?

For most people, of course, this is merely a description of what, as analysts, they are already doing. After all, no one likes to think of themselves as imposing an authoritarian order; and no psychotherapist would want to see them-selves as suppressing conflict. And there are also further puzzles in all this. Because the implication – which is so vivid in a political context – is that the more authoritarian the regime, the less conflict is permitted, but the more it is cultivated. The conflict is with the authorities, with the ones who are supposed to know. In other words, would a democratic psychoanalysis end up as, or begin as, a conversation between equals? Because the advantage, the beauty so to speak, of the one who is supposed to know, is that what he knows suppresses conflict. He can tell us the truth about ourselves which will apparently dispel the rival truths. Instead of having to conciliate rival claims on ourselves – by ourselves and others – we can attain a superiority of knowledge.

From Bion's small, potentially leaderless groups to Lacan's professionals whose superiority to their interlocutors is guaranteed in advance to Chantal Mouffe's democracy that depends on conflict, on agonistic pluralism; in each case something about equality is being contested, something about its provenance and its value. As though a great deal might depend upon finding a good description of it. As though we are not sure whether equality as an ideal is our most pernicious mystification, or one of our best inventions. And perhaps one useful – usefully circumscribed – way of looking at it is through the issue that has haunted and informed the history of psychoanalysis: the equality, or otherwise, of the analyst and the unfortunately named patient. If he is a patient, the analyst is a doctor; if he is a client the analyst could be a solicitor; and if he is a lost soul the analyst is a member of the third of Lacan's professions based on superiority. So what, in the abstract, could be described as being equal about the analyst and the person with whom he will have what Lacan calls a psychoanalytic experience, a psychoanalytic opportunity? And why, if at all, would it be better to think of them, in any senses, as equals? What are they equal to, and what might they be equal for?

III

... a common ear for our deep gossip
Alan Ginsberg, 'City Midnight Junk Strains'

Psychoanalysis as a treatment and an experience, like democracy as a political process, allows people to speak and to be heard. Indeed it encourages people to give voice to their concerns, to be as difficult as they can be, because it depends upon their so doing. Of course lawyers and priests and doctors also require that people speak of their discontents. But they expect people to speak, or listen to them as though they are speaking with deliberate intent and with a view to decision. After such conversations, ideally something specific will be done. And even if the kind of democratic forums we are familiar with are less overtly specialised – and even if they encourage dissent and debate and competing accounts – they press for some kind of consensus with a view to significant action. A democracy may consist of doctors and lawyers and priests, among others, but each of these individuals may be more or less democratic, more or less free to be democratic, in their practice. Expediency doesn't allow for endless debate. The idea is not to sit around all day having interesting conversations, and entertaining points of view. It is with a sense of some kind of urgency – with a sense of something being at stake, of something that can't be set aside or ignored – that people enter the political arenas, and consult their respected professions. Similarly, people don't seek out psychoanalysis, even if they think they do, or would like to, for a bit of armchair philosophy (indeed, from a psychoanalytic point of view there is no such thing as an armchair philosopher, there is only the negotiation of distances). Presumably all cultures

15

provide settings or forums, places people can go to and people they can go to with their most intense feelings, their most urgent dissatisfactions. Whatever troubles people, and they can't talk themselves out of, seeks expression.

One way of talking about this is in terms of what people recognise as a solution. And to talk about solutions – and whether solution is the word at all – is to talk about forms of satisfaction. Democratic process, for example, may not be simply the best way of making decisions, or of conciliating rival claims; but the being in a democratic forum – hearing all those voices, in oneself and others, being drawn out by contact with all those speaking bodies – may itself be a kind of happiness. Or not, as the case may be. If, as Stuart Hampshire says in *Justice in Conflict*, 'The value of a democratic constitution lies in the defence of minorities, not of majorities', and that 'Even the fanatic who is sure that he knows best in discriminating justice from injustice also knows that he must prepare himself with arguments to meet disagreement', then disagreement is taken for granted. Or, to put it differently, disagreement – with oneself and others – never comes to an end; but an end, more or less provisionally, can be put to it. What is difficult about some versions of psychoanalysis and some versions of democracy is that they value disagreement as much as, if not more than, the solutions it occasions. Indeed, from a psychoanalytic point of view, disagreement is itself a solution. Violence can be the attempt to make disagreement disappear. And it is, of course, the violence people do to themselves and others that the psychoanalyst hears so much about. Psychoanalysis investigates what people can say without the relief of violence.

There is on the one hand the need to make decisions, to have a capacity for choice; and on the other hand there is the willingness to sustain disagreement. And choice, of course,

without conflict, without competing alternatives, is nuga-
tory. There is only choice when there are things to choose
from. And this, again, I think, is where equality comes in. If
choice and conflict are inextricable, the conflict only exists as
such because the conflict is in some sense between equals.
And equality here doesn't mean sameness; it means
differently appealing but equally compelling good things.
Desiring ones mother and desiring ones father; wanting to
be independent but needing to be attached; wanting to be
excited and wanting to be kind; both have much to be said
for them. They can either be usefully sustained as conflicts,
or the conflict can be suppressed by authoritative imposition. I can become unassailably either heterosexual or
homosexual; I can be invulnerably arrogant or abjectly
needy; I can become more or less sado-masochistic; I can
become altruistically ascetic or brutally promiscuous. I am
not suggesting, of course, that these are ever, or ever could
be merely (voluntaristic), conscious decisions; but they are,
in overly schematic form, the conscious and unconscious
self-fashionings that we come across in this culture, in
ourselves and others. The aim of psychoanalysis, one could
say, might be the precondition for democracy; that a person
be able to more than bear conflict, and be able to see and
enjoy the value of differing voices and alternative positions.
That a person might want to confer some version of equal
status on the conflictual voices that compose and discom-
pose him. We could then say, for example, that most people
are homosexual and/or heterosexual until or unless they
meet someone who makes them feel otherwise; that our
bisexuality is waiting to happen, so the most interesting
thing about one's so-called sexual identity would be the
surprises it springs rather than the programmes it entails.

And from this point of view aggression would not be seen

simply, or merely, or solely, as some kind of innate, quasi-biological essence. It would be seen as, or also seen as, the voice called up in the self to put a stop to conflict. Aggression would be seen to be creating a certain kind of conflict as a way of suppressing vital conflict. The analyst, like the democrat, would be attentive to – would be vigilant about – attempts to suppress both the possibility and the sustaining of conflict within the individual and the culture. The analyst would position herself as a democrat, wherever the so-called patient placed her through the transference. So in my version of analytic neutrality, neutrality would never be the right word; because to think of oneself as neutral in a democracy doesn't make sense. It would only make sense that the analyst would be finding ways of sustaining the conflict that is a form of collaboration, that democracy speaks up for. The analyst, or the whole analytic setting, would be like a rendezvous for the conflicts entailed by the refusal, the suppression, of conflict.

The analyst would be wanting to be, in other words, the opposite of Winnicott's definition of a dictator in his *Some Thoughts on the Meaning of the Word Democracy*. 'One of the roots of the need to be a dictator', he writes, 'can be a compulsion to deal with this fear of woman by encompassing her and acting for her. The dictator's curious habit of demanding not only absolute obedience and absolute dependence but also "love" can be derived from this source.' The dictator is, as it were, the ultimate version of the figure Lacan refers to, whose superiority to his interlocutors is guaranteed in advance; and in this sense democracy is the heir of the Oedipus complex because the couple are exchanged for, are replaced by, the group; fascism is the triumph of the couple, of the dictator and his people.

Psychoanalysis has always been involved, one way or

another, in the war against dictatorship; in the difficulty, if not the impossibility, of equality between people (and within people). If for Winnicott the meaning of the word democracy takes him straight back to the meaning of the word 'motherinfant', it should also take us back to the meaning of the word psychoanalysis. After all, from a psychoanalytic point of view it would not be surprising to find – whether or not individual psychoanalysts think of themselves as democrats – that the battle between dictators and equals has always been fought out in every area of psychoanalysis; from the teaching of it to the practice of it. And it has, perhaps, been exemplary as a profession in the way that it has kept the whole question of superiority – of the nature of prestige and dictatorship – on the agenda. Issues to do with equality are never far away when psychoanalysis is discussed, celebrated or disparaged.

IV

Efficient practice precedes the theory of it.
Gilbert Ryle, *The Concept of Mind*

If one wanted to reflect on psychoanalysis and democracy – on psychoanalysis and the meaning of equality – it might seem sensible at first to give some definition of democracy, but the difficulties of doing this are instructive in themselves. And it is worth remembering that democracy, like psychoanalysis, is a quite recent phenomena. 'Until half a century ago', the political theorist Larry Seidentop writes in *Democracy in Europe*,

democracy was a word unknown to most of the non-Western world. Even in the West, until two centuries ago, the word carried decidedly unfavourable connotations. Until then the role of the idea of democracy was not unlike the role of the id in Freud's theory of the psyche – both suggested a dark, inscrutable and fathomless threat from below. The upper classes of European society and the established churches looked upon democracy as something almost demonic.

It is, of course, interesting that he should have recourse here to Freud's id by way of analogy and comparison. The threat posed by democracy was to assert that certain kinds of liberty, and certain kinds of satisfaction, were not reserved for the privileged. It is curious, if we read the analogy both ways, to think of the ego and the super-ego being somehow akin to the aristocracy and the church. And yet when Freud showed us how what he called the ego was no longer master in its own house, or that the ego drove the horse in the direction the horse wanted to go in, he was intimating something similar. As though the id was the new, alter-native, previously repressed voices which either are sexual and aggressive, or are described as sexual and aggressive to represent their primary quality, which is to be disruptive of the previously established order. Something else was demanding its right to be represented and heard. And put like this, the psychoanalyst is both herald and sponsor of the new democratic world.

It is very clear and entirely appropriate that the nature of democracy has been greatly contested. In Seidentop's view, democracy evolved from Christianity with

the assumption that we have access to the nature of things as individuals. That assumption is, in turn, the final justification for a democratic society, for a society organised to respect the equal underlying moral status of all its members, by guaranteeing each 'equal liberty'. That assumption reveals how the notion of 'Christian liberty' came to underpin a radically new 'democratic' model of human association.

It is the valuing of the individual despite his social status, and not because of it, that both Christianity and democracy promote. It is as though people are deemed to be something – to have something inside them – that is of equal value; and of a value greater than any worldly assessment can encompass. It is paradoxical that what exempts people is the ground for their inclusion. And it is, inevitably, the forms of equal liberty and the nature of this supposed 'underlying moral status' that have been, and are, ultimately contentious. What, I think, is less debatable is that there has been 'a radically new democratic model of human association'. More people associate with, have access to more kinds of people from different classes and countries and histories now; and they associate with these previously isolated others from a quite different position. Some of them, for example, may assume that despite their manifest differences from these other people they have some other things – perhaps more important or 'deeper' things – in common. And the keyword, as it is for psychoanalysis, is association, as the way into something new. Indeed the only time the word 'free' ever gets used with any kind of regularity in psychoanalysis is with reference to free-association, in which words are encouraged to consort with each other to unpredictable effect. Psychoanalysis, like democracy, works through the encouragement and validation of new forms of association and the conflicts they inevitably reveal. To have an appetite for association – of a political or psychic kind – is to have an appetite for, if not to actually seek out, fresh forms of conflict; and to see conflict as the way we renew and revise our pleasures. Democracy, one could say, extends the repertoire of possible conflict. It fosters an unpredictability of feeling and desire. It makes people say, or people find themselves saying, all sorts of things to each other.

When Chantal Mouffe says that 'for democracy to exist, no social agent should be able to claim any mastery of the foundation of society,' I take her to mean that there can be no superordinate expert, nobody tuned in to the real or true nature of things (as a dictator would claim to be), because there is deemed to be no real, or true, or absolute foundation of society. Indeed it would be a monarch, or a dictator, or an aristocracy, or a church who would represent themselves as essentially the representatives and the masters of the foundations of a society. And the notion of a social agent mastering the foundations of society is not worlds apart from Lacan's account of those whose superiority to their interlocutors is guaranteed in advance. Because democracy, in Mouffe's version, doesn't provide foundations in that sense – ones that can be mastered – it is again similar to psychoanalysis; whose paradoxical foundation is the unconscious, which by definition is not subject to mastery, even if what it is subject to is always in question. The new, both similar and different, kinds of association promoted by psychoanalysis and democracy are not, though – or not only – ends in themselves. What, after all, is all this new association in the service of? Is it merely a way of enlarging the market? How does it bring us the lives we want, and what is it about these particular lives that we do seem to prefer? We may not want to be so overtly dominated by absolutist tyranny, or corporate enterprise, but what do we want these new kinds of conflicts to do for us?

If it is perhaps more obvious what these forms of free association are freedom from, it is less clear what they are freedom for. Free association, in a psychoanalytic context, is designed to reveal the strange orderings of unconscious desire. 'When conscious, purposive ideas are abandoned,' Freud writes, 'concealed purposive ideas assume control of the current of ideas.' Freedom from censorship is freedom for the disclosure of unconscious desire. And desire, one could say, is always desire for exchange. Or, if one wanted to put it a little more circumspectly, one could say desire is always a person's question about exchange. Freud's 'conscious purposive ideas' could be translated as the accepted entitlements of those with status, and 'concealed purposive ideas' could be read as the voices of the subordinated. Freedom from acknowledged forms of regulation is freedom for economic and erotic exchange. What proliferates is proliferation itself. The reaches of appetite can be explored. And in providing a setting for such freedom – and in defining a space as being for this and nothing else – what is so quickly revealed are the obstacles to free-association, the difficulties, the hesitations, the pauses, the knots and shames and ruses that occur, and occur to someone when they are encouraged to speak.

When Ferenczi said the patient is not cured by free-association, he is cured when he can free-associate, he was acknowledging the very real difficulty everyone finds in sustaining and making known an internal democracy. People literally shut themselves up in their speaking out; speech is riddled with no-go areas; internal and external exchange, as fantasy and as practicality, is fraught with resistance. Psychoanalysis reveals just how ambivalent we are, to put it mildly, about freer forms of association (from a psychoanalytic point of view there is no such thing as a free enterprise). And this must surely be where the analyst comes in. If the so-called patient is deemed to be suffering from one form or another of association-anxiety, presumably the analyst has something up his sleeve, so to speak, for precisely this predicament.

Encourage the patient to free-associate, Freud says; call

this the 'fundamental-rule' of analysis and what will come to light, in detail, are the patient's misgivings about doing this. Let someone talk and they will start showing you that they can't; and how they can't. They are always, in Chantal Mouffe's words, from a quite different context, 'suppressing [conflict] by imposing an authoritarian order'. And, in all probability, delegating to the analyst this thankless task of ordering them about. In this sense psychoanalysis reveals – whether or not the analysand recognises himself as a democrat, as someone who professes democratic rights and obligations – the anti-democratic voices and urgings, and their complex history. And as anyone knows who has had a psychoanalytic experience there is often a great and shocking immediacy to these unconscious authoritarian impositions of order. One can't help wondering just what conflict is experienced as such that it calls up such violent hatred. The protest against, the hatred for – not to mention the desire and longing for – the figure whose superiority to his interlocutors is guaranteed in advance must be as nothing to the agonies and terrors of conflict. As though the alternative to there being a subject supposed to know, rather than a subject who can only live his dividedness by not trying to abolish it, is felt to be catastrophic. So what can the analyst do, where can she put herself, so to speak, to make conflict – and the pleasure conflict involves – the desirable and desired state of being? How does one acquire a taste for democracy, a desire for democratic values?

John Dunn begins the Preface to his book of essays, *Democracy, The Unfinished Journey: 508 BC to AD 1993*, with the words:

This is a book about the history and significance of an old but vigorous idea; that in human political communities it ought to be ordinary people (the adult citizens) and not extra-ordinary people who rule. This is not a very plausible description of how things are in the world in which we live. But it has become the reigning conception today across that world of how they ought to be. The idea itself is devastatingly obvious, but also tantalisingly strange and implausible.

The idea of something at once devastatingly obvious and also tantalisingly strange and implausible is as good a definition as any of what used to be called making the unconscious conscious. That which has been rendered unconscious tends to have an elusive strangeness, even uncanniness about it; and is both hard to believe and hard not to. And yet here, of course, John Dunn is talking about an idea of political community and organisation called democracy, which Dunn's faintly amusing subtitle points to as having been something of a long-term struggle; that is to say, as something with potent adversaries and enemies.

The whole notion of extending effective political power to more and more people; the idea of people having a right to choose their own government and, in some sense, rule themselves by themselves – by their own consent – without the need for people (or deities) of extraordinary and superior status; this, as an ideal and a political struggle, turns the world upside down. And it does this in part by making new kinds of association between people both possible and necessary. The whole idea of an extraordinary or superior person, or group of people, has to be re-described. The old tautologies – the King is superior because he is the King – no longer hold. Hierarchy becomes a matter of consensus rather than divine or any other kind of right. Agreement and disagreement have a whole new status; they become the new effective currency of political life (democrats are not magicians). And psychoanalysis, of course, has something to say, or something to add, about the causes and reasons of agreement and disagreement; about the function of the agreeable and the disagreeable in people's lives.

From a psychoanalytic point of view this has to do with the inequalities – for want of a better word – that human development involves and entails. The gist of this might perhaps be captured in the absurd question: what would it be for a child to be the equal of its parents? What might there be in this obvious but also tantalisingly strange and implausible question that might be cause for resistance? To identify with democratic values and institutions requires, among many other things, that children no longer need, for their psychic survival, to think of their parents (and so of anyone else, including, particularly, themselves) as extraordinary or superior creatures. In psychoanalytic language, the enemy of democracy is not so much admiration as idealisation. And this means, in Chantal Mouffe's terms, that it is essential to the viability of democratic values that they are not themselves idealised. Stories about equality, stories about self-government, stories about consent are there to be continuously reconsidered, not fixed (or reified) by idealising them (the whole notion of mastery being both the cause and the consequence of idealisation). If we speak in the psychoanalytic way of mothers and fathers and children, the democratic idea and ideal of people's right to choose and participate in their own government comes out as, however consciously or unconsciously conceived, people's right to choose their own parents and siblings. I cannot choose my parents – my family and its histories – but I may be able to choose the form of government I live by. It is obvious why for some people – and perhaps for most people some of the time – democracy can seem unnatural and transgressive. We don't speak enough, in other words, of democracy as a forbidden pleasure. And if we were to do this, we would get a clearer sense of the profound ambivalence in psychoanalysis about democratic values; an ambivalence reflective of, or simply of a piece with, this same ambivalence in the wider culture, of which psycho-analysis is always a part.

When I was training to be a child psychotherapist about twenty years ago we were asked by the committee running our course for suggestions about what we would like to be taught. When some of these suggestions were turned down, and some of us got rather cross, we were told by a member of the training committee that 'children can't bring them-selves up'. As it happens I was a child then, but some of my contemporaries were in their thirties and forties, and had children themselves. So unsurprisingly, perhaps, they were rather affronted and bemused by this. It is integral to the point I want to make that, in retrospect, I think of this as an emblematic story about ambivalence, in both parties, about democracy; about the anxieties of equality. To be told either rather abstractly or rather dogmatically that sanity depends upon acknowledging and respecting the difference between the sexes and the difference between the generations doesn't always clarify this issue. Because the issue is: what kind of equality is viable in the light of difference?

It is peculiarly difficult to produce descriptions in psychoanalytic language – from a psychoanalytic point of view – of equality. Or rather of what kinds of equality might be emotionally viable for people rather than just more spurious ideals, or too-wishful propaganda. All versions of psychoanalysis are informed by the relative helplessness and dependence of the human infant, the centrality of the Oedipus Complex, and the excessive power and logic of unconscious thought and desire. All this provides at best a sense, to use Dunn's phrase, of an unfinished journey in psychoanalytic theory and practice towards any feasible ideas of equality, or indeed of freedom.

It would be extravagant to say that psychoanalysis is essentially a story about why equality is impossible for human beings. But in the most cursory reading of Freud, Klein or Lacan, equality, in any form, doesn't spring to mind as a keyword. If psychoanalysts are mindful of the ways in which people are not equal to being themselves, not equal to the task of living; are unable, or unwilling, or overly enthusiastic about treating others as equals; if psycho-analysts tend to produce accounts of what people are really like that stress desire, dependence, greed, rivalry and abjection, the question of equality, in one way or another, has arisen around issues of treatment and training. All analysts agree, though they have different ways of saying this, that people are split subjects; but people are not assumed to be, as it were, equally split. All analysts agree that everyone has or is an unconscious; though people are not assumed to be, as it were, equally unconscious. But when it comes to training and treatment these issues become particularly pertinent.

Though training and treatment, as in all professions, are inextricable, I want to concentrate by way of conclusion on the question of the connection, if any, between equality and psychoanalytic treatment – a connection that would have to be privileged if there could ever be a democratic psycho-analysis. Or rather a psychoanalysis that declared itself as democratic in intent. And by that I mean a treatment that saw itself as being about, whatever else it was about, the difficulties every person has in identifying with democratic values. Psychoanalysis of course was not conceived as, is not supposed to be, a political training camp; but that it has pretended not to be one, that it has at its worst created the illusion that it is possible to exempt oneself from group life, from politics, has, I think, been more damaging and misleading than need be. All social practices transmit preferred values. So just to localise the larger question, I want to ask in what sense it may be useful or true, or useful and true, that there is any equality between analyst and patient. And I don't mean by this that some kind of equality is the aim or the consequence of a good psychoanalytic experience; I mean, what kind of equality could be considered as a precondition for a democratic psycho-analysis? What would it mean – both for psychoanalysis and for the so-called treatment – for the analyst to assume, at the outset, any kind of equality between herself and the patient? Treating someone as an equal, as psychoanalysis shows so well, is not as simple or easy or uncostly as it might seem. But then, not treating people as equals is also its own kind of prophecy, its own kind of project.

There have, of course, throughout the history of psycho-analysis been various statements by psychoanalysts – Ferenczi, Winnicott and Laing among others – to the effect that the analyst and the patient are above all two human beings. Though sometimes saying this doesn't quite say enough; or rather it begs the question that needs to stop begging and being begged. 'A sign of health in the mind', Winnicott writes in a paper called 'Cure',

is the ability of one individual to enter imaginatively and accurately into the thoughts and feelings and hopes and fears of another person; also to allow the other person to do the same to us ... When we are face to face with a man, woman or child in our speciality, we are reduced to two human beings of equal status.

The idea that when we are face to face we are two human beings of equal status leaves open the question of when we are not face to face, when one person is on the couch, facing away. The phrase 'two human beings of equal status' requires us to describe what this equality could consist of, just where it might be located. It is interesting that Winnicott's sense of equal status overrides here the differences between the generations and the sexes: 'When we are face to face with a man, woman or child ... we are reduced to two human beings of equal status.' But why is 'reduced' the word here? Because it is akin to one of Freud's antithetical words meaning at once diminished and re-stored? Winnicott implies that the equality resides in each person's ability – though freedom would be a better word – to 'enter imaginatively and accurately into the thoughts and feelings and hopes and fears' of another person; and, as integral to this, to have the freedom to 'allow' the other person to do this to oneself. This reciprocal entering into, this mutual intercourse between people that he sponsors here is, at least in a psychoanalytic context, a radical new form of association. It implies that the analyst allows himself to be, for want of a better word, known by the so-called patient. It would be the mark of Lacan's professional whose superiority to his interlocutors is guaranteed in advance, that he would have to set certain kinds of limits to intimacy. Like Rickman's definition of the neurotic who is ego-centric and loathes collaboration, this person has always decided beforehand, however unconsciously, on the nature of the exchange that will take place. The entering into of each other will be severely regulated. What Winnicott doesn't tell us – and it seems rather important in the context, though also perhaps forbidden to broach – is how this mutual imaginative intercourse is compatible with psychoanalytic practice, with the gathering of the transference.

In the more democratic forms of analysis it would be assumed that the analyst and the analysand need to find ways of knowing each other – or experiencing each other – such that the idea of the superiority of either of them disappears. It ceases to be relevant to the matters at hand. Because superiority – as Lacan's respectable professional and Rickman's neurotic make clear – is a function of distance. In a more democratic psychoanalysis the aim is to transform superiority into useful, or bearable, or even pleasurable difference. But perhaps this need not be merely the aim of psychoanalysis, so much as the precondition of its possibility. The analyst, that is to say, starts from a position – a listening position – in which there is no such thing as superiority because there is nothing to be superior about. And that, of course, is as much to do with his manner – who he happens to be and happens to want to be – as to do with his so-called technique. Indeed the whole notion of technique, at its most extreme, is complicit with fantasies of superiority.

If we think of psychoanalysis as a listening cure, as an agreement that two people will bear together the consequences of their listening (to themselves and each other), we could then start wondering about something I want to call free listening, in counterpoint to the notion of free speech. We could think of psychoanalysis as an enquiry into the equality of listening; into the senses in which we can be equal to what we hear. And into what we might do when we are not.

On Being Laughed At

*... laughing at the same jokes is evidence of
far-reaching psychical conformity.*
Freud, *Jokes and their Relation to the Unconscious*

One of the oddly striking things about Primo Levi's initial impression of Auschwitz, which he describes in the first fifty or so pages of *If This is a Man*, is his sense that this must be some kind of joke. On entering the camp, he writes:

They make us enter an enormous empty room that is poorly heated. We have a terrible thirst. The weak gurgle of the water in the radiators makes us ferocious; we have had nothing to drink for four days. But there is also a tap – and above it a card which says that it is forbidden to drink as the water is dirty. Nonsense. It seems obvious that the card is a joke, 'they' know that we are dying of thirst and they put us in a room, and there is a tap, and *Wassertrinken verboten*. I drink and I incite my companions to do likewise, but I have to spit it out, the water is tepid and sweetish, with the smell of a swamp.

The scene has a kind of archetypal resonance; they are thirsty but they cannot drink. And it is Levi's instinct, so to speak, to work out why people would do such a thing. He is in search of an explanation for something unbearable, and the idea he comes up with is that the card itself must be a joke. The water is surely fine, but the sign is actually the sign of someone's sense of humour. It must be a joke for Levi because the world can't be this incoherent and cruel; if people are thirsty no one shows them a tap and says, but you mustn't drink the water. In short, it is a joke for Levi because it is so cruel; and because it must be a joke, it can't be true. So he drinks the water and it is so disgusting he has to spit it out. The sign is telling the truth; and it is there, in a certain sense, to protect them. Why did it occur to Levi to think of this as some kind of joke? And the answer is that he believes that there are people who might play such jokes on others, but there can't be such people in the world who would refuse people water for four days and then put them in a room with a tap they can't drink from. In other words, there is something about human cruelty that Levi cannot imagine. And of course, something else about human cruelty – the joke – that he can. People can joke about such things, but they could never do them. As he intimates, the joke was on him. But it is the joke that is Levi's preferred form of explanation; that there are jokes and jokers in the world makes this experience, at least initially, intelligible to him.

If jokes and mockery are one motif in his grave and horrifying book, the other motif is to do with teaching and learning, as though there are two ways Levi organises his experience: on the one hand there is mockery, and on the other hand there is something we might call, for want of a better phrase, moral education. When Levi is not describing the ridicule of camp experience, he is using the language of pedagogy ('One learns quickly enough to wipe out the past and the future when one is forced to'). In Auschwitz, Levi is at once a student of human experience in extremity, and the object – both in reality, and in his own interpretation – of an unbearable, an inconceivable taunting and teasing.

The camp, in Levi's account, is, among other things, a

kind of anti-university, a brutal parody of humanistic learning. 'We have learnt other things, more or less quickly, according to our intelligence,' he writes, 'to reply jawohl, never to ask questions, always to pretend to understand.' What you have to learn is obedience; inequality created and recreated through intimidation. If the sign on the tap is an answer there is no need for a question. The joke is the last-ditch explanation before the questions begin. Levi cannot even pretend to understand what is happening to him: 'I have stopped trying to understand for a long time now'; and clearly, by the same token, 'they' are not trying to understand him:

Some more hours pass before all the inmates are seen, are given a shirt and their details taken. I, as usual, am the last. Someone in a brand new striped suit asks me where I was born, what profession I practised 'as a civilian', if I had children, what diseases I had had, a whole series of questions. What use could they be? Is this a complicated rehearsal to make fools of us?

They are asked questions, but cannot ask them – except, as Levi does here, in their minds. And once again, out of his general bewilderment he wonders, and it is another question, whether what they are really doing is making fools of them. 'For many weeks', he writes of the signs around the camp, 'I considered these warnings about hygiene as pure examples of the Teutonic sense of humour.' Shaved – 'What comic faces we have without hair,' Levi remarks – there is another shower ordeal; and Levi asks one of the officials what has happened to the women, will they see their wives and daughters again. 'Certainly we will see them again,' the man replies; 'but by now', Levi writes, 'my belief is that all this is a game to mock and sneer at us.' Levi keeps coming to the conclusion that the only way of explaining this deranged and brutal world

to have been made by people – tells us that we have the capacity to make choices. Determinism tells us that we are punished for things we are unable to choose not to do.

To describe someone as inhibited is to assume – at least in this particular area of their lives – that they are not the victims (or the beneficiaries) of an absolute determinism. That for reasons of which they may be largely unconscious they have chosen to do one thing rather than another; to go to bed with someone, say, but not to have sex with them, to go to a party, but not to mix in. They are, in Moore's terms, acting according to preference. So to understand something about inhibition, we need to say something about the nature of preference. Because at its most minimal, preference implies a sense of purpose, a project (however unconsciously conceived); and a sense of satisfaction in the offing, of moving towards our pleasure, even if one of our pleasures is safety, or frustration, or uncertainty. To fail at one thing is to succeed at another, and vice versa.

But in an essentialist theory like psychoanalysis – a theory which already knows what we are most likely to be inhibited about or around – what we have failed to do tends to be privileged over what we have succeeded in doing. Is the impotent man, for example, more failing to be fully sexually alive than, say, succeeding at eliciting sympathy or dismay from his partner? In other words if we are to describe inhibition in terms of preference – as I think we must – we are likely to get bogged down in preferring some preferences to others. To tell a persuasive story about inhibition we need to be as imaginative about its hidden successes as we are about its more vivid failures. And if we do this what is more often than not disclosed is a complex array (or disarray) of projects afoot. There is something strangely reassuring about witnessing the familiar parade of one's putative failings. The free will that inhibition entails is a complicating factor. Not only are there two things we might have done, one of which we have chosen; there is also the many things we are doing or intending to do in doing one and not the other. Inhibition turns out to be an exhibition of more than we realised. In our inhibitions – in the areas of our lives where certain things seem impossible – we are over-achievers. We are doing too much where we seem to be doing so little.

IV

To taste the pleasure one is giving would be to violate
as grave a taboo as that of incest.
Denis Hollier, *Absent without Leave*

Freud's title *Inhibitions, Symptoms and Anxiety* (1926) seems to propose a kind of causal chain: we suffer from an inhibition of a vital practice (something supposedly normal becomes impossible), we develop symptoms, and we suffer from anxiety. Freud defines an inhibition here as 'the expression of a restriction of an ego-function'. And what he means by an ego-function, broadly speaking, is what Rado meant by useful healthy activities carried out by normal people, which Freud lists as 'the sexual function', 'the function of nutrition', 'locomotion' ('a disinclination to walk or a weakness in walking'), and work. And these restrictions, he suggests, are the consequences of a person's attempt to avoid conflict.

Inhibition is a person's cure for conflict. If this particular activity became a possibility an unbearable conflict would ensue. Whether, in Freud's language, the ego represses sexual desire to avoid punishment from the super-ego or further assault from the id; or whether, in what he refers to as 'more generalised inhibitions' – as happens in mourning, or the management of excessive feeling or overpowering sexual fantasy – in which the 'psychical task' involves so much energy that a person is inhibited through sheer depletion of energy, either way a particular course of action is prevented. 'As regards inhibition,' he writes, 'we may say in conclusion that they are restrictions of the functions of the ego which have either been imposed as a measure of precaution, or brought about as a result of an impoverishment of energy.' Inhibitions protect one from danger and exhaustion. They are self-preservative: conservative not innovative.

As so often with Freud's writing, this account of inhibition sounds like a version of common sense. To be uninhibited, in certain areas of one's life, would feel like being unprotected. It would be like making oneself available to danger. It would be like being too freely associated with one's instinctual life – and therefore too involved with others – and it might, as over-exertion, literally extinguish one's energy. And yet the question in the background – the consideration that makes this kind of language intelligible – is, what would it be like to be disinhibited? What might actually happen, what would one find oneself feeling? At its most minimal, Freud intimates, one precondition for being uninhibited is being able, being, as it were, more than willing, to bear conflict. As though one might come to see that the value, the point of being able to bear conflict is that one can be less (and not more) inhibited. And it is not only, or just conflict the uninhibited have to bear; it is also the possibility of being suffused with feeling, or what Freud calls 'a continual flood of sexual fantasies'. This is an interesting phrase in that presumably a *continual* flood ceases, eventually, to be called a flood, and becomes, say, a lake, or a river. In other words, following the image, sexual fantasy would become in time no longer invasive or overwhelming; it would be just what we were, what was in our minds, or just what our minds were. It would not be alien, but integral. The imagined uninhibited life would be a radical metamorphosis. We would no longer feel flooded, we would be a flood.

Indeed, it is sexuality, as usual, that provides Freud, in *Inhibitions, Symptoms and Anxiety*, with his most vivid examples of neurotic inhibition. And strangely, they echo the juxtaposition in the poet Kenneth Koch's life of writing and treading on people: though in Freud's example, it is a mother, not a baby, that is stepped on:

As soon as writing, which entails making a liquid flow out of a tube on to a piece of white paper, assumes the significance of copulation, or as soon as walking becomes a symbolic substitute for treading upon the body of mother earth, both writing and walking are stopped because they represent the performance of a forbidden sexual act. The ego renounces these functions, which are within its sphere, in order not to have to undertake fresh measures of repression – in order to avoid a conflict with the id.

One version of common sense might say: writing and walking could become even more enticing, even more irresistible, having been sexualised. But of course, if the sexual is the forbidden – or always has an insistent echo of the forbidden – then that is exactly where we are likely to hesitate. So inhibition occurs, for Freud, when any action is contaminated by, or unconsciously likened to, forbidden sexuality. In this view we are never out of control, or indeed losing control, we are more or less doing forbidden things. And when we inhibit ourselves – which we often refer to as controlling (or over-controlling) ourselves – we are in fact choosing safety in preference to transgressive excitement.

But there is a bind here which could be crudely stated as: why bother to write if it doesn't in some way feel sexual, if it doesn't smack of risk-taking? If we take the forbidden out of the picture there's no keen edge, no passionate necessity to our excitement; but if we put too much forbidden in – if writing becomes incest in our minds – we are stopped in our tracks. The inhibited person, we might say, can't take on the forbidden, can't face it; so at its most extreme everything is safe, but there is no anticipation; there is certainty, but there is little suspense. Inhibition, once again, as a form of omniscience.

Put like this, what I am saying begins to sound like a rallying cry, as if we should just all be a bit braver. And yet one of the many merciful things about psychoanalysis as a therapy is that it doesn't tend to make appeals to what used to be called the will. Indeed, to think of will-power as the cure for inhibition would be a perfect example of what Leslie Farber called, in a memorable phrase, willing what can't be willed. So if inhibition is all to do with the forbidden, and we can't have a will-full relationship to either inhibition or the forbidden, what can we do if a greater degree of freedom is one of our aims? Clearly, how we describe the forbidden will dictate what kind of relationship (if that's the right word) we can have with it. And Freud tells us that any activity – or 'function', to use his scientific term – has to feel sufficiently forbidden to be of genuine appeal to us; but it must not seem too forbidden or we shall be paralysed. If we were to speak in the absurd language of quantity we would say, when it comes to the forbidden we have to have just the right amount.

To think about the forbidden is to wonder, or perhaps remember, what parents seem like to children. And to wonder about the limits of redescription. From a brashly pragmatic point of view we could, for example, simply say that the forbidden is just something we haven't yet been able to describe in a way that makes it accessible. Along the lines of my earlier discussion, it would be that the inhibited person keeps describing certain of his activities in ways that make them too terrifying to enter into. Freud's writer insists – consciously or unconsciously – on describing writing to herself as copulation, so of course she mustn't do it. So as happy pragmatists we can say: she needs both a new description of copulation and then, maybe or maybe not, a new account of writing. In other words, it isn't the writing that's the problem, it's whatever she – in unconscious fantasy – thinks is going on in intercourse that's inhibiting her. For the happy pragmatist – about whom I do not feel facetious – the only problem about sex is the way we describe it. In childhood – for all sorts of reasons that psychoanalysis can help us with – we come up with the wrong stories about sex. We really begin to live as if sexuality is, say, a torture chamber, a devour-and/or-be-devoured orgy, a mutilation, an endless game of hide-and-seek, and so on. We are inhibited; we cannot possibly prefer the frightening representations we have found for whatever it is that goes on between people when they are intensely (and intently) drawn to each other. Or we are so excited, or so shamefully excited by these lurid options, that we have to refuse them in order to sustain a preferred image of ourselves that seems essential to our very being. Because when we are talking about inhibition we are also talking about the kinds of people we want to be and fear turning into. As Alex Coren has said, can we imagine being the kind of person who could be anything? To think about inhibition is to think about the constraints on self-fashioning, on self-invention.

And yet most of us will have a strong sense that it just isn't as simple as this, and I think we should be more curious, more genuinely perplexed about why it isn't this simple. Or what we might need to add to the pragmatist's account to make it sound more convincing. Anyone who has experience of psychoanalysis – and perhaps of other forms of therapy – knows that both the analyst and the patient can come up with a very good, facilitative redescription of an inhibition and that it can be either resisted by the patient or, more interestingly, accepted by the patient (if not actually considered to be something of a revelation) and still not make a blind bit of difference. An inhibition is always an inhibition until it isn't one. We are talking about the feeling of not being able to do something; of the act of preferring, and the sense of impossibility.

When there is something we can't consent to ourselves doing, we must have a belief that we could do it if certain conditions prevailed, if there could be guarantees, as it were, that in the doing of it, certain feelings would not be felt. Rado's 'impossible' refers, I think, to whatever must not be felt. If I do the thing I can't do, certain feelings will be repeated, or at least disclosed, that I assume (perhaps rightly) that I cannot or must not be able to bear. Whether it is about incapacity – I actually don't have the equipment, the wherewithal to feel these feelings – or whether it is about permission – I can't allow myself to be the kind of person who feels such things – is not always clear. To have the courage of one's preferences is to have the courage of one's feelings. Every wish is an experiment in consequences.

V

*The real is the only thing in the world we can never
get used to.*

Clement Rosset, 'Reality and the Untheorisable'

In cognitive terms one could describe inhibition as the inability to believe something about oneself; to believe, say, that one could be the kind of person who could feel such feelings, or carry out such acts. And this links the experience of inhibition with the more pervasive experience of not being able to believe in something; and especially not being able to believe in something that one should be able to believe in. I am thinking, for example, of the many powerful nineteenth-century narratives of people unable to believe in God any more, or unable to accept the religious observances of their families. And there is a difference, of course, between losing a faith one has acquired and being unable to acquire this faith in the first place (in psychoanalytic language it is the difference between illusionment and bearing disillusionment). What was then called the spiritual struggle of the protagonists of these dramas – as in Froude's Nemesis of Faith, say – is usually posed as a question: is it an incapacity, or is it a refusal in the hero that he is unable to believe? And if it is not, then, what we might call an inhibition, what else could it be? Is impotence – to take a secular, more carnal analogy – a new version of the self, or merely a fear? Is it a resistance, or a revision of the self, and how are these two things different? I am putting it in this more cognitive, more sensibly intelligible way to draw attention to the difficulties of putting it more psycho-analytically. And by psychoanalytically I mean closer to the confounding irrationality of feeling inhibited, of being patently and unavoidably divided against oneself. Unable, that is, to will oneself out; knowing what the wished-for good is and unknowingly (or, unconsciously, *too* knowingly) preventing oneself from attaining it. What, in other words, would be a good psychoanalytic description of what, in more traditional language, would be called a crisis of belief? A situation in which it is not just that someone cannot, or can no longer believe in God, but that he can no longer believe in himself as a believer? If I am unable to believe in something – unable to perform something like a belief or a sexual act, unable to believe in or imagine myself doing such things – I might ask myself, in a psychoanalytic way, what pleasures are being courted or compromised, what punishments are being sought and averted in my being like this. And yet, even put like this, it sounds very close to a certain version of behaviourism. To find what I would think of as the psychoanalytic thing – the object, for want of a better word, of specifically psychoanalytic acknowledgement – we have to find what is, as it were, insolubly irrational about inhibition. We have to be able to render something intelligible – find a useful and interesting redescription of it – without rendering it only intelligible. Or, to put it another way, we have to redescribe it in a way that shows it to be subject to further – unknowably further – redescription.

What I make of my inhibition will be different at different times; that is, I will be using it to make different kinds of future possible at any given moment. I am saying this at such tedious length because I think inhibitions are spectacular – are central to psychoanalysis in the way Rado emphasised – because on the one hand they seem only to be intelligible by presupposing an unconscious; and yet the unconscious disclosed by psychoanalytic accounts of inhibition too often seems just like another consciousness, a hidden one. As though we have two minds for the price of one. We want one thing, but unconsciously we want something else, and we want it more; and what we actually do reveals what we actually want. As though our wants are not so much irrational as unacceptable. All the analyst has to do is show the patient the multiplicity of his competing, and mostly hidden wants. And perhaps also, ideally, to show the patient how such wants have come to seem, or indeed to be, unacceptable. Then the patient can evaluate his wants; the lights go up in the supermarket and he can choose. Where once he hesitated, now he can consume. Inhibition as a complaint – my sense of my own unfreedom, my sense of self-imposed restriction – could, in other words, make us too pragmatic in our apprehension of ourselves; too knowing of what we want; too incorrigibly rational in the way we figure the future.

VI

*Cruising, like sociability, can be a training in
impersonal intimacy.*
Leo Bersani, 'Sociability and Cruising'

Psychoanalytic theory always deduces a rationality from irrationality; what looked as though it was excessive, obscured or unintelligible turns out to be, becomes explicit, if not entirely explicable. And this, of course, should give us pause. All versions of psychoanalysis tell us that we are not as opaque as we thought we were, or that we are not opaque in the ways we thought we were. Descriptions are available to us that can leave us less puzzled. The drift towards clarification – however sophisticated in its theorising or glib in its acknowledgement of mystery – might make us wonder what a psychoanalysis would be like that sponsored neither the good sense of the ego nor the brash moralism of the super-ego; nor took flight into an idealisation of the id. Surrealism is so easily tedious because it so quickly seems like more of the same. And being rude and cruel are not, broadly speaking, impressive ideals. In the different immersion experiences provided by the different schools of psychoanalysis – with their different stories about the past, childhood, sexuality, development, not to mention the unconscious – an interesting dilemma keeps resurfacing when people start discussing the so-called aims of analysis. And it can be simply stated as a question: is the aim of psychoanalysis to make people kinder, or to make them more unpredictable?

Some people – many people – would say that the aim of analysis is not to *make* people anything but, one way or another, to let people be who they are; to find out the more about themselves that they have needed to not notice. I think people are always making themselves and other people into something; that psychoanalysis itself is a story about how we are made up, and how we are – albeit unconsciously – making up our lives. And that psychoanalysis, by its own definition, could not be the place where this stops. The analyst and the so-called patient are, among other things, wanting to persuade, and more indeterminedly, influence, each other (as do parents and children). And as the aims of psychoanalysis are always a reworking of – and so a reflection on – the aims of child-rearing we return to the original question. A question, as I say, that a parent as well as an analyst might ask: is the aim of psychoanalysis to make people kinder, or to make them more unpredictable? And just before we sensibly say both, it's worth noticing that unpredictability and kindness have, as philosophers say, quite different entailments. Or, as *we* might say, this is rather more complicated than it looks. We might, for example, think that we know what being kind involves; but we know what unpredictability involves in a quite different sense. Our own and other people's unpredictability does something to us that our own, and other people's kindness, doesn't. Perhaps we can get the gist of this if we imagine what our lives would be like if we preferred unpredictability to kindness; or if, in any given situation, we intended to do the kind thing rather than the unpredictable one. Inhibition, I want to suggest, is a crisis of unpredictability, in which questions of kindness are never far away.

Clearly, what it is to be kind is every bit as contentious as what it is to be unpredictable (as the idealisation and the use of the word 'spontaneity' always reveals). And yet, 'be kind' is not so much of a double-bind, so to speak, as 'be unpredictable'. And 'be unpredictable' is often the frightening injunction the inhibited person is giving himself (or giving other people in the hope that they might free him). Indeed all the psychoanalytic diagnostic categories describe ways which people have found of being predictable to themselves, despite themselves. That's what a symptom is; it's a repetition, an unconsciously motivated self-prediction (and by the same token, the 'patient' in psychoanalysis is cured when his past is no longer of particular interest to him). At best we flirt with our own unpredictability through our symptoms; at worst we are over-contained by them. Inhibition stages this as a drama. It is not always, or only, the inability to do something; it is also a cover-story, a protection against, not quite knowing what it is one wants to do. And what one might turn into, what one might feel, in the doing. The inhibited person, that is to say, has the most acute sense of the experimental nature of our acts. Of how doing something, doing anything, consigns one to the future, to the irreversible. To a future of unknown feeling; to the shock of the unprecedented.

Inhibition at its most minimal, one could say, is a kind of doubleness; and from a psychoanalytic point of view its ultimate referent, its centre of gravity, is the forbidden. What I want to do that I cannot do – what my preferred self would be capable of – either I must not do (because it is forbidden), or I am quite literally unable to do (I don't have the capacity for). I may be inhibited about public speaking, but I cannot honestly say that I am inhibited about choreography. What we tend to call inhibition has something to do with realistic possibility; but in a way that what we call unconscious fantasy does not. Indeed the irony of it is that the inhibited person has managed to transform the possible into the impossible, the realistic into the utterly implausible. In its most benign yet tantalising form, the difficult act is imaginable; at its most extreme, it may be literally unthinkable. That, the inhibited person says to himself, is a pleasure only for others: they will have to do it for me. But what is most striking is the tyranny of the relationship with the other who can perform the forbidden act. The doubleness of inhibition, in other words, could be described as a sado-masochistic relationship with the self; an internal problem that is unusually suited to, and suitable for, public performance. Indeed, at its most extreme, the inhibited person begins to have his primary relationship with his imaginary uninhibited other. A game for two that only one can play.

From this point of view the uninhibited one is a gleeful, sadistic triumphalist. He is only uninhibited as part of a more pressing project, which is to make the other masochistic one feel abject and inhibited. And by the same token, as it were, the inhibited masochist goes on failing to perform to make the relishing sadist feel potent and pleasured. Because of the collusive mutuality of this deadly pas de deux neither must be seen to be ultimately succeeding (the sadist never kills the masochist, if he can avoid it, because then he will lose the game that sustains his identity). It must always seem slightly possible and virtually impossible that the feared act could be performed (sado-masochism, that is to say, is a perversion of hope). The sadist tempts and mocks the masochist with the forbidden act, and the masochist consents to his oppression and absurdity. What is sustained is the paradoxical sense that a choice is being made in a situation in which there is really no choice. In fact the whole notion of choice seems like a spurious fiction, a lure invented by a sadist; the sadist says, you can choose to do what you want to do, and the masochist finds that he can only choose what he doesn't seem to want to do. The sadist says, of course you can make choices, but you are only able to choose what you least want; the sadist says, of course people choose what they want, but they don't really know what they want. And the masochist says, glumly, or ironically, or bitterly, what I seem to really love is my own frustration; the self I like to keep fashioning is an abject, self-depriving one.

In this variation of the Faustian pact – in this sado-masochistic loop, this closed system – it is often the sadist that chooses the objects of desire so as to better stage the humiliation. What is being so well arranged is a familiar kind of frustration. And I think it is worth stressing just how well-managed these scenarios usually are, however uncon-scious a person is of what they are doing. Indeed one of the things one might be doing in analysis is showing the so-called patient just how he goes about choreographing his favourite dispiriting drama.

But, of course, the crucial 'how' question is usefully shadowed by the 'why' question. Why would someone go on doing such things? The answer will be different for each person, integral to each person's different and always differing history. And yet it may be possible to say something more general in scope, that can be useful when it is made particular. This great unkindness, this inventive cruelty to oneself always has one overriding consequence; it renders a person apparently predictable to themselves. The shy person will always either not go to the party, or go to the party and suffer. What is then occluded, what is concealed or even supposedly abolished, is the unpredictability of the self. Where unconscious desire was – the person risking themselves in the search for pleasure – there an (albeit abject) surety will be. Where there was contingency, there will be repetition. Where there was a text, there will be a set text. Inhibition – the whole sado-masochistically staged drama of it – is like a ruse of the ego in its relentless project of negating the unconscious. Like a charm or a spell, the endlessly compelling sado-masochistic project – with its virtually mechanical forms of reproduction – distracts a person from the only freedom they have, the freedom to choose an unpredictable future for themselves.

UNDER PSYCHOANALYSIS

Around and About Madness

*A chain of associations is to him what a chain
of reasoning is to other men; and what he calls his
opinions are in fact merely his tastes.*

Thomas Babington Macaulay, 'Southey's Colloquies',
Edinburgh Review, 50 (January 1830)

When the British psychoanalyst John Rickman – who was,
not incidentally, a Quaker by upbringing – remarked that
madness is when you can't find anyone who can stand you,
he was asking a couple of questions. Firstly, what makes us
feel that we can't stand someone? And this becomes, for the
sake of diagnosis as it were, a question about how we know,
about how we describe what it is about them that we can't
stand. And secondly, what do we tend to do when we can't
stand someone? Answers to the second question constitute
what we now call the history of madness, which is more or
less a history of fear, at least in the modern era. A history of
forms of classification; and of how the so-called mad create
an unease that cannot be ignored, and for which they have
often been punished by the state, and other bystanders.

The hatred of this unease has sometimes needed explaining – and hatred itself always makes us fearful – but the mad
have traditionally been those people we have to do something about. It has been assumed that, like criminals, we
must do something with them or they will do something
with us. Unlike criminals though, they are not always

people who have committed crimes. They are either felt to be harmlessly strange – withdrawn, out of reach, out of touch; or gifted; or potential criminals, capable, perhaps, of crimes we have never even dreamed of. But in so far as they don't break the law – it's not, for example, against the law (yet) to hear voices or not to speak – they are more like people with disturbingly bad manners. People who, by not playing the game, make us wonder what the game is. And indeed why the rest of us have consented to play it. So the mad have also been available to idealise as cultural outlaws or odd prophets, as though madness was a glamorous misery and not a monotonous one. As though to be treated as an oracle was not itself a form of scapegoating. What we call madness – like what we call pornography – is that which we cannot remain indifferent to. It is, in other words, something about which everyone has or takes a position.

So there is a certain relief (along with the terror) when the mad commit crimes, or when the criminal is described as mentally ill, because then their behaviour seems intelligible, straightforwardly transgressive rather than horribly eccentric. The law (like medicine) is always trying to keep up with the mad, keep track of them – and modern political regimes (like modern psychiatric approaches) have shown just how easy it is to recruit the language of mental health for diverse political objectives – because those people referred to (however loosely) as mad are always people who seem to be unable or unwilling to follow rules. Their language, their beliefs, their bodily gestures, their hygiene, their hopes and expectations can be wildly at odds with some putative norm. They remind us of what it is to be normal. As Rickman's comment suggests, what is called madness is all to do with sociability, and what sociability is all to do with.

Whether it is bandied about by anti-psychiatrists or by anti-democrats, the word madness covers what would once have been called a multitude of sins. But at its most minimal it is always pointing out the same thing: something so unacceptable about a person (or a group of people) – either to themselves, or to others, or to both – that intervention seems to be required. So-called madness can be described as a message, always enigmatic and always disturbing, that creates a certain kind of environment around itself (a world, say, of fearful, dismayed, punitive people; a world of curious, protective, kind people, and so on). It is defined, so to speak, by what it elicits in others. It feels like a call to action; at one end of the spectrum there is the silencing and segregation of the mad, at the other end there is the treatment of the mad that is, at least in intention, more sympathetically disposed. Madness may be treated as a call to action but this action even at its most well- (or ill-) intentioned cannot simply or solely be described as relief from suffering; because to relieve someone of their suffering can be to deprive them of their point of view (to think of suffering as the worst thing we suffer from can itself be a form of censorship). There is the suffering of the supposedly mad, and the suffering caused by the mad; and the pervasive difficulty of working out who is doing what to whom. Or rather, of working out which kinds of conflict we can bear to value. This, as Rickman intimated, is to do with the consensus in any given society about what are considered to be the valuable pleasures.

The word mad is normally used about someone when their sociability begins to break down, but in a way that seems to endanger sociability itself (no one understanding what someone is saying, everyone feeling intimidated by someone). Just what it is that madness seems to endanger –

how these forms of classification, these rhetorical terms and figures operate in a given society – is what the mental-health professions have to account for in order to justify their existence. Talking about madness, in other words, is a way of talking about our preferred versions of a life; of what it is about ourselves and our societies that we want to protect and nurture (if we can), and what it is about ourselves and our societies we would prefer to be rid of (if we can). So the political implications of the concept and the category of madness – the consequences of speaking the diagnostic languages of mental health rather than more simply saying who we are prepared to listen to and why – seem self-evident. And yet there are always going to be people who feel more comforted and consoled – more understood, i.e., part of the group – by being diagnosed, by being subject to apparently authoritative descriptions. It is always a mixed blessing to resist the solace of sociability. If diagnosis is the problem and not the solution, if it is merely, as it were, legitimated ganging-up, then those who are to resist it will need powerful counter-descriptions of their own. The question is always going to be, from where can they get the words they need, from whom can they get the emotional buoyancy that will free them to speak? It is about whether people can make any kind of group out of whatever it is that isolates them. All forms of political oppression are ways of isolating whatever is threatening them. So it always looks like a conundrum: are people mad because they are isolated, or are they isolated because they are mad? Are people different because they are oppressed, or are they oppressed because they are different? The answer is clearly both, but it is the momentum of this vicious cycle that is horrifying for all concerned.

Every culture has its own ways of taking people seriously,

and of telling what is serious about people. And Western cultures in the modern era have institutions to train people in the forms of recognition the culture wants to promote. So there are people who know what art is, people who know what illness is, people who can decide what it is to break the law, and so on. And yet the category of madness has always been a problem wherever legitimation has been an issue. Around and about the enigmas of legitimation – who legitimates the legitimators; which people, or how many people, have to agree to make us believe that something is good, or true, or real, or beautiful – what has been called madness has been whatever has put legitimation procedures into doubt (in *The Bacchae*, as in *King Lear*, a mockery is made of what people most believe in). Madness is that which disrupts due process as defined by the powers-that-be; and exposes the fact that the powers-that-be are not the only powers-that-be. It becomes the category – of thought, of feeling, of desire, of drama – that none of the categories can contain. And it crosses the disciplines, so to speak, by blurring their concerns. Whether madness is a legal issue or a medical issue; whether it requires a scientist or an artist to make it intelligible; whether indeed the artist or the scientist (or the serial killer) in some sense need to be mad to be who they are and do what they do; all this makes the concept of madness akin to the universal acid of (scientific) folklore. That there could be something in a culture – call it a force, or a voice, or an energy, or a figure – that nothing and no one in the culture can command. And that it might always be baffling whether this something was a source of renewal or a source of ruin, so that no one would ever be able to tell whether this was a good or an evil thing, a thing we should worship or a thing we should deplore. These are the once-theological preoccupations that the secular notion of madness keeps in circulation. Madness becomes a way of talking about what is wrong with the ways we describe what is wrong with us. It reminds us, in a technological age – rather like the body, or the notion of the unconscious – that the fact that we can describe ourselves doesn't mean that we invented ourselves. That there is more to us than we have been able to account for, and that this more may be precisely what we should pay attention to. Though not, perhaps, in the way people previously payed attention to God (or the gods). When people are being excessive, we can call them mad; that is, when they are being excessive about the wrong things.

And yet what all the exhilarating talking (and writing) about so-called madness tends to discount – madness as demonic and chthonic; madness as parody and inspired critique – is the misery of it. And, secondarily, the very real difficulties – difficulties of terror and of comprehension – of being, in any capacity, with very disturbing people. Glamourising the mad may at least have encouraged people to consider the possibility of listening to people they would rather flee from; but it also idealised certain forms of suffering in a way that was sometimes unrecognisable to the sufferers. Treating people as special is often a way of neglecting them. And this is where politicising the mad and describing political dissidents in the language of mental health is pernicious. The mad are like the politically oppressed in so far as they can be the victims of a powerful consensus that needs to invalidate them; the politically oppressed are like the mad in so far as they are punished for their beliefs (their actions and their sentences). The mad are unlike the politically oppressed in so far as they may be destructive in ways they themselves can't bear and which isolate them in ways they can't bear. The politically

82

SKIP AHEAD
12 LEAVES (24 PAGES)
TO GET TO PAGE 83

oppressed are unlike the mad in so far as what makes them political is that they share their beliefs with at least some other like-minded people. In short, the politically oppressed are always a group; the mad often aren't – at least from their own point of view. As Rickman intimated, you aren't mad, or you aren't that mad, if there are people who can stand you. In political groups there are often people who admire and believe in each other. Clearly the vilest political regimes destroy the opposition by most cruelly isolating them; either from the outside world, or from each other, or from both.

If the mad are traditionally those people in the culture who make inadmissible connections – who live as if they are like Napoleon, who link life with excess (of strangeness, of silence, of coherence and incoherence) – they are defined by their capacities for recruitment. When they organise certain groups of people against themselves – in our culture, psychiatrists and sometimes the police – they are called mad; when they organise other kinds of people around them, speaking on their behalf as it were, they are called religious (or cult) leaders, politicians, celebrities, or very (and variously) talented people. People are not called mad when sufficiently influential people agree with what they are saying. Once one takes seriously the extent to which consensus is sovereign in matters of so-called mental health, as in so much else, one realises just how endangered any individual or group of people is once they put themselves out of range of the available, culturally sanctioned descriptions. At its worst, the mad, like the politically dissident, are prevented from adding to the stock of available reality. And it has, inevitably, been the official languages for managing the mad that have regulated their contribution; that have more or less decided where and how they can participate in the lives of those deemed to be full of mental health.

If for the sake of discussion – but not necessarily for the sake of justice – one blames neither the psychiatrists nor the mad for what they have done with each other, it is possible to see that, broadly speaking, there are two modern accounts of madness. In one account, which the big money is on, what we call madness is an organic (neuro-logical, genetic) disfunction of the organism. The mad are MADNESS chronically maladapted bodies; they need a combination of #ONE rewiring and new chemistry to regulate, if not to cure, the destructiveness of their natures. At the extreme end of this spectrum they were born with this madness – call it schizophrenia, call it bi-polar disorder, call it depression – in their bodies. At the less extreme end something was done to their relatively normal bodies – call it a traumatic experience, a war, an illness – and it deranged the physics and chemistry of who they were. Science, which by definition understands such things, has a lot to say about this bit of the physical universe. From a scientific point of view these things are thought of as disorders rather than complaints; though this, in and of itself, doesn't make a scientific approach less compassionate. But it does assume some kind of knowledge, some kind of picture of what it is for an organism to be well-functioning. And the mad, whatever else they can do, are not good at functioning. Or at least at functioning as previously defined. The first Christians, like the first trade unionists, were obviously proposing new ways in which people might function. But of course, from the scientific psychiatrist's point of view the person diagnosed as schizophrenic is not inventing a new way for people to live, he is unable (or failing) to live in the normal way. Indeed he needs to get back to that putatively normal state so that he is in a position to choose whether he wants to be a Christian, or to join a trade union. Mad bodies are ill-equipped, or just not ready for human culture. In this view, at its most extreme, the mad are not makers of meaning; they don't have the equipment for it. So, a bit like children, they are the beneficiaries and the victims of other people's meanings. They have descriptions foisted upon them from a (consensually agreed) more privileged position. Clearly, what the mad are deemed to be like – animals, children, machines which have broken down, eclipsed geniuses – will dictate how they are to be treated.

In the other modern account, madness is described as a person's ingenious though debilitating self-cure for the obstacles thrown up by his individual development. And as all development is deemed to be traumatic these mad solutions will turn up, to a greater or lesser degree, in everyone's life (these solutions are normally called a person's character). Or madness is taken to be just a description of what human beings really are. In the depths, in our hearts, as passionate creatures we are mad; in excess of the cultures we create, and always beyond our most searching descriptions of ourselves. In this view, who we are is a mockery of what we make, because who we are is fundamentally uncontainable (all our cultural forms are just ways of getting away with something). The notion that we are truly and deeply mad is, of course, far older than the notion that, given a chance, we are eminently sane. But in these accounts it is our nature to be mad, and it is our nature to protect ourselves from this madness (which psychoanalysts, for example, call desire or instinctual life). And the ways we have found to protect ourselves or cure ourselves – called defences, or symptoms, or eccentricities – are themselves mad. Madness, in short, is considered to be both the problem and the solution. So the sponsors of this account are always, one way and another, trying to make a case for some kinds of madness being better than others; the madness of sexual love for example is preferred to the madness of agoraphobia, or obsessive-compulsive working habits, and so on. But whichever madnesses are given credit, they are all assumed to be either utterly, if obscurely meaningful; or indeed to be the very source of meaning, as though what we call madness is the matrix of all our sense-making. And what we call reason is just part of our madness, one of the many things our madness has come up with: our rationality as ventriloquist's dummy of a more startling irrationality.

Madness as source, and madness as dysfunction are unpromising options. And it has become reasonable these days, when it comes to what was once called madness, to prefer more complex descriptions of whatever it is about other people that disturbs us and them. Ideally these descriptions combine rather than simply exclude the available methods and knowledge. And yet, of course, being reasonable about madness is at once all we can ever be – the most radical anti-psychiatrist, like the most radical biological psychiatrist, must by definition have their own shareable logics, their own persuasively cogent arguments – and the most implausible thing we can be. All writing about madness is either proud or embarrassed about its distance from what it describes. Whether one writes deliriously or dispassionately about madness one cannot escape a binding paradox: if it can be represented (described), in what sense is it madness? If it can be represented – in psychiatric diagnosis, in political character assassination, in lyrical description – why call it madness rather than strange (or unacceptable) behaviour? Why not, for example, attempt, without prior categorisation, increasingly nuanced and subtle descriptions of unusual ways of being a person? Instead of bestiaries we might just have collections of tales.

The reason this may not happen is that, in actuality, madness is the word we use to refer to the violence we most fear; and so, by implication, to talk of madness is to talk, however obliquely, of whatever it is in ourselves and our societies that we dread being violated. It is the violence – real and imagined – that the so-called mad do to us, or to something about us, that is likely to make us cruel in return. It is both the drawback and the advantage of the scientific approach to madness that it starts from the position that we (the sane, the doctors) can transform them (the mad, the nominally ill), but they must not transform us. And yet from the other point of view I sketched above – call it the bohemian approach – wherever the nature of an exchange has been decided in advance there is something called oppression at work. This is why the scientists are often more politically co-optable than the bohemians by the more repressive regimes.

It would be nicer and better if we stopped thinking in terms of reason and unreason, stopped working out who is mad and not, and started working out who we are prepared to listen to, and why; and, of course, what we imagine the consequences of such listening might be. But we would have to do this mindful of the very real terrors involved, and so be able to distinguish, as far as is humanly possible, between punishing people and looking after them (doing either in the name of the other is a mystification). That the language of so-called mental-health experts has been so easily recruitable for nefarious ends should make us wonder whether these really are the best descriptions available for the most extreme forms of modern suffering.

If you can't find anyone who can stand you, you can't find anyone who believes you've got anything they want.

Groups consist of people who, for better and for worse, need each other's company. What we call madness highlights our infinite anxieties about exchange with other people. The anxiety of influence is as nothing compared with the anxiety of exchange.

The Soul of Man under Psychoanalysis

I

One walks about the street with one's desires,
and one's refinement rises up like a wall whenever
opportunity approaches.

T. S. Eliot to Conrad Aiken, 31 December 1914

Writing a 'London Letter' for the *Dial* in August 1922, Eliot suggested that there were 'at present ... three main types of English novel'. There was the 'old narrative method', the traditional tale, represented by Wells, Bennett and Compton Mackenzie. And at the other end of this contemporary spectrum was the 'dangerous' Dostoyevskyan novel in which the writer has what Eliot calls 'the gift, a sign of genius in itself, for utilizing his weaknesses'. Dostoyevsky, in Eliot's view, has a relationship to his own pathology that is a form of artistic vocation. 'Epilepsy and hysteria', Eliot writes, 'cease to be the defects of an individual and become – as a fundamental weakness can, given the ability to face it and study it – the entrance to a genuine and personal universe.' The idea that what one is suffering from, that what one experiences in oneself as weakness or defect or shame might be 'the entrance to a genuine and personal universe' sounds, of course, like the kind of thing Freud and his various inheritors were saying at around this time. That symptoms of illness were signs of meaning; that personal vulnerability was an opening – an 'entrance' to use Eliot's word – that where people were vulnerable was where they had once made room for other people. For Eliot, 'the most interesting novelist in England' is D. H. Lawrence, who has, in his view, been 'affected' by Dostoyevsky.

And yet sandwiched between the conventional and the Dostoyevskyan novel there is what Eliot calls 'Another interesting type, but of a very short ancestry ... the psychoanalytic type'. Ancestry was, as we know, very important to Eliot. Psychoanalysis itself – a 'scientific method', Eliot writes, '[that] rests upon a dubious and contentious branch of science' – was very new at this time (the British Psychoanalytic Society was set up in 1919). So the whole notion of a psychoanalytic novel was of an unprecedented type. This type of novel, 'most notably illustrated' by May Sinclair's *Life and Death of Harriet Frean*, was not, in Eliot's view, promising. 'The conclusion of Miss Sinclair's book', he writes,

... extracts as much pity and terror as can be extracted from the materials: but because the material is so clearly defined (the soul of man under psychoanalysis) there is no possibility of tapping the atmosphere of unknown terror and mystery in which our life is passed and which psychoanalysis has not yet analysed.

Extracting pity and terror in obedience to Aristotle suggests something at once willed and formulaic about Sinclair's novel. But the allusion to Wilde's *The Soul of Man under Socialism* is perhaps more telling in this context. Neither Wilde nor Freud, for quite different reasons, were ever Eliot's cup of tea. Indeed they both seem to represent for Eliot false solutions to a similar problem, the problem of evil. Psychoanalysis and socialism, not to mention Wilde's particular brand of flagrant theatricality, were for Eliot a patently inadequate response to Original Sin. 'For ... the men of the 'nineties,' Eliot wrote (in *For Lancelot Andrewes*),

Evil was very good fun. Experience, as a sequence of outward events, is nothing in itself; it is possible to pass through the most terrible experiences protected by histrionic vanity; Wilde, through the whole experience of his life, remained a little Eyas, a child-actor.

It is that something is being treated with insufficient seriousness; whether it is the excessive clarity of Sinclair's psychoanalytic novel – 'the material is so clearly defined' – or the excessive, hedonistic self-regard of Wilde's 'histrionic vanity', some fundamental experience is being alluded to, in Eliot's view, without the appropriate gravity. It is what he calls 'the most terrible experiences', 'the atmosphere of unknown terror and mystery in which our life is passed', that he needs to find the language for. And clearly it cannot be found in the dubious science of psychoanalysis, and was evaded in Wilde's amused child-acting. 'On the other hand,' Eliot adds to his uneven-handed appraisal of Wilde, 'even to act an important thing is to acknowledge it'; but it was the important thing that mattered to Eliot, and the important thing was Sin. Eliot predicts that 'Miss Sinclair will find herself forced to proceed from psychotherapy even to the supernatural'; because, presumably, you can't get at – through psychoanalysis, in the language of psychoanalysis – the important thing that Sinclair is deemed to be gesturing at.

The phrase 'the soul of man under psychoanalysis' tells us, perhaps better than any elaborated critique, where Eliot stood in relation to the ambitions of psychoanalysis; both what he saw these ambitions as being, and how he saw them as operating. Where once, from a theological point of view, there was Sin, there was now, from a socialist point of view, exploitation and class war; and from a psychoanalytic point of view, instincts and incest. The soul of man under psychoanalysis, in other words, was deemed to be suffering from a secular form of self-division. What Eliot calls in *Notes Towards the Definition of Culture* 'higher religion', 'imposes a conflict, a division, torment and struggle within the individual'. 'In the higher religion,' he writes, 'it is more difficult to make behaviour conform to the moral laws of the religion.' For Freud, it is one's instinctual nature in its definition by culture that creates 'a conflict, a division, torment and struggle within the individual'. It is notable that the language of the experience is the same – conflict, division, and struggle (torment perhaps has a rather different inflection) – but the source is relocated, and the conflicting agencies and forces are redescribed by Freud in secular, quasi-scientific terms. Where Eliot describes his 'higher religion' as 'imposing' this conflict, this division for the redemption of the soul, Freud found that his patients were the casualties of imposed ideals; that higher religions – in their various modern secular and sacred guises – were what people were now suffering from. Their supposed nature was irredeemably at odds with their cultural ambitions for themselves. They couldn't, in Eliot's words, make their behaviour conform to their moral laws. Their symptoms were the sign – the attempted self-cure – for the impossibility of this project.

The 'fundamental weakness' that Eliot saw Dostoyevsky as so successfully transforming into great art was sinfulness; for Freud the source of Dostoyevsky's great art is captured in the title of his paper of 1927, 'Dostoyevsky and Parricide'. This, one could say, would be a kind of glib shorthand for the differences between them. And yet Freud and Eliot, with their quite disparate personal and cultural histories – Freud a godless European Jew and Eliot a gradually aspiring American Anglo-Catholic – have what might be called a shared perplexity, an anguished scepticism about the self. They are both preoccupied by how modern people render what is unacceptable about themselves intelligible; the preconditions for recognising something as unacceptable, and the nature of an adequate response to it. That we are divided souls – if not actually divided selves – is not in question for either of them. What is in question is finding the suitable, the sufficient language for this conflict, this division, this torment and struggle within the modern individual.

When Harold Bloom writes with his useful (and usual) fervour about Eliot that 'To have been born in 1888, and to have died in 1965, is to have flourished in the Age of Freud, hardly a time when Anglo-Catholic theology, social thought and morality were central to the main movement of mind,' he is writing with unnecessary triumphalism. The whole idea of 'the main movement of mind' is, after all, as precious to Eliot as it is to Bloom. If in some spurious, putative cultural competition the language of Freud has won over Eliot's language of Anglo-Catholic theology; if some or many or most of us are more likely to talk about sexuality, violence and childhood than about the soul, original sin and redemption when we talk about people now, it is surely worth remembering just what this transition from the language of sin to the language of unconscious, incestuous desire entails. It is naive to believe – as both Eliot and Freud showed us in their different ways – that languages could ever be anything other than the traces of their own histories. We would be right to assume that there were continuities and evolutions where there seemed to be ruptures and revolutions. That in speaking (and writing) a language we enunciate our histories. And both Freud and Eliot write out of a history of descriptions of self-division; of the individual in conflict, riven in one way or another. It is no accident, so to speak, that Laing took his title *The Divided Self* from William James's *The Varieties of Religious Experience*.

It is one thing to suffer from a sense of unease or anguish, but it is quite another thing to organise it into a conflict. The whole notion of conflict implies powers of discrimination; the ability to judge, for example, just what it is about one's nature that is sinful. For there to be a conflict of any sort there has to be a separating out of forces, recognisable differences. You can't have a war if you don't know who the enemy is. In other words, conflict and self-division – as descriptions of what is going on inside ourselves, and between ourselves and others – depends upon a high level of intelligibility. When I identify a thought or a feeling or a gesture as sexual; when I feel bad about my unkindness, it is as though I have understood myself. To be ashamed of oneself is to be in a state of total conviction; a state of conviction so absolute that it would seem impossible and silly to wonder just how one had acquired such certainty about the nature of one's actions. It is shocking to realise just how opportunistic one's scepticism can be. Our scepticism seems to be no match for our self-punishment, or indeed our punishing of others.

If, as seems to be the case, we take self-division, we take conflict for granted – as Freud and Eliot clearly do – and if we take seriously the problem, and not merely the progress, of secularising a language, then the question becomes, is this division, this conflict we experience in ourselves, a revealing of our sinfulness, and if not, what is it revealing of? It may be revealing just of the fact of division or conflict itself – the setting up of oppositions, the sorting out into adversarial or competing positions – or it may be a self-cure for excess, the excess of feeling and desire; and yet so much depends upon the way in which we assign moral status to the combatants. In this agonostic picture of ourselves – by which we are clearly compelled if not actually bewitched – there is an anxiety about the division of the moral spoils. Once we relinquish the reassuring but sparse intelligibility of a world of goodies and baddies we begin to experience the vertigo, the disarray of what is politely called moral complexity.

When we don't understand something – and especially when we have taken understanding to be our currency – we are prone to coerce and oversimplify. 'It is human,' Eliot writes, using the difficult word,

when we do not understand another human being, and cannot ignore him, to exert an unconscious pressure on that person to turn him into something that we *can* understand: many husbands and wives exert this pressure on each other. The effect on the person so influenced is liable to be the repression and distortion, rather than the improvement, of the personality; and no man is good enough to have the right to make another over in his own image.

Perhaps it is too Freudian to say that Eliot's stated dislike of Freud was an inverted affinity; but the language here – unconscious pressure, repression and distortion of the personality – and elsewhere in Eliot's prose, is more than merely allusive. And running the psychological account into the overtly religious, 'no *man* is good enough to have the right to make another over in his own image', dramatises the collision and collaboration of languages that is integral to my subject. But more importantly for my purposes here, I want to read Eliot's description from what could be called a psychoanalytic point of view, and say that it is also an account of the unconscious pressure people put on themselves when they don't understand themselves. That what Eliot thinks of here as an inter-psychic pressure – something going on between people, and perhaps couples in particular – is also an intra-psychic pressure; something we do to ourselves when our unintelligibility to ourselves makes us suffer. We make ourselves apparently familiar to ourselves. And what else, we might wonder, could we possibly do? This, I take it, is one of the dilemmas that psychoanalysis sets out to explore. People come for psycho-analysis because there is something about themselves that baffles them and that they cannot ignore (to use Eliot's word). This is the quotation from Eliot, rewritten:

It is human when we do not understand ourselves, and cannot ignore ourselves, to exert an unconscious pressure on ourselves to turn us into something that we *can* understand: many husbands and wives exert this pressure on each other. The effect on the person so influenced (oneself, that is) is liable to be the repression and distortion, rather than the improvement of the personality; and no man is good enough to have the right to make another over in his own image.

Eliot is writing of the human fear of not understanding something or someone that is human. He is saying – in his version and in mine – that when we cannot understand another person or ourselves we put pressure on them, one way or another, to become something we can understand; and that this pressure is the kind of influence that represses and distorts. As though there can be an anxiety about not understanding those people – including oneself – that one cannot ignore. And not being able to ignore someone – or not being able to ignore something about oneself – is itself a kind of revelation of character. In a sense, we are what we are unable to ignore. And what we do with what we cannot ignore is, of course, at the heart of psychoanalysis.

Eliot is a writer fascinated by what he cannot understand, by the limits of intelligibility, by the obscurity of experience. 'The world, as we have seen,' he writes in the Conclusion to his Harvard dissertation on F. H. Bradley, 'exists only as it is found in the experiences of finite centres, experiences so mad and strange that they will be boiled away before you boil them down to one homogeneous mass.' This acknowledges both the recondite eccentricity of personal experience, and its irreducibility to a system. There is something, even the young Eliot believed, about experiences so mad and strange that by definition, as it were, resist explanation. So when he writes of May Sinclair's novel that 'the material is so clearly defined (the soul of man under psychoanalysis) there is no possibility of tapping the atmosphere of unknown terror and mystery in which our life is passed and which psychoanalysis has not yet analysed,' it is more than implied that psychoanalysis has not yet analysed this atmosphere, and will never be able to. Because this unknown terror and mystery, these experiences so mad and strange, are not subject to anything we can call analysis. As he writes tartly in his dissertation, 'For a metaphysics to be accepted, good-will is essential.' Assent is generous bad faith.

Experiences so mad and strange, unknown terror and mystery, can be addressed and described in both secular and religious terms. What Harold Bloom calls so tendentiously the Age of Freud is better known as the period in which more and more people in Europe were moving over to a secular, at least quasi-scientific account of what had been traditionally religious concerns. Previously, what was unintelligible in experience had been referred to God. For Freud, among many other people of the time, the unintelligible was referred to materialism, and more specifically to the body in culture; and to what bodies could do to each other, and why they did it (Darwin, of course, is one of the central figures here). What couldn't be understood in human experience found a new set of referents. Freud was not talking to his patients (or to his colleagues) about their souls and their relationship to God, he was talking to them about their bodies and their relationships with their parents; and above all, about their relationship to their spoken (and unspoken) words. In this medical context, experiences so mad and strange were called symptoms; and the therapeutic project was to find forms of understanding that made a difference. The psychoanalytic conversation, such as it was, was about personal history rather than religious observance. What Bloom refers to, with perhaps a bleak irony, as flourishing in the Age of Freud, meant no longer seeking religious solutions for the problems people saw in life. But it is the fate of the unintelligible – of that which cannot be ignored and cannot be understood – that preoccupies Eliot and Freud, among others, at this time. The mystery in life either needed a new referent, or people needed to be reminded, in no uncertain terms, of its traditional, sacred referent.

II

Act in such a way that I can speak to you.
Maurice Blanchot, *Awaiting Oblivion*

There is a dramatic moment in Eliot's essay of 1951, 'Virgil and the Christian World', when it is as though Eliot is looking both ways at once. He is in the process of discussing the question of whether Virgil's fourth eclogue was in fact a prophetic text; prophesying the coming of Christ, as some later commentators were to insist. 'Whether we consider Virgil a Christian prophet', Eliot writes,

will depend upon our interpretation of the word 'prophecy'. That Virgil himself was consciously concerned only with domestic affairs or Roman politics I feel sure: I think that he would have been very much astonished by the career which his fourth Eclogue was to have. If a prophet were by definition a man who understood the full meaning of what he was saying, this for me would be the end of the matter. But if the word 'inspiration' is to have any meaning, it must mean just this, that the speaker or writer is uttering something which he does not wholly understand – or which he may even misinterpret when the inspiration has departed from him. This is certainly true of poetic inspiration.

The question is how we understand the meaning Eliot gives to the word 'inspiration', a word he uses very sparingly in his prose, as one might expect (there are only eight references cited in his other writing, and they are all in his plays). If poetic inspiration comes from God, from Eliot's Christian God, so to speak, then it is as though Virgil, in this case, may not understand what he is writing but God did and does, as do Virgil's later Christian commentators. Prophecy, after all, is not so much to predict the future, but to foretell it, to know what will be called history in advance. The mystery would be that the poet, Virgil, could write at once so knowingly and so unknowingly.

And yet if we take Eliot's definition of the word 'inspiration' away from Virgil's pagan (or proto-Christian) world and Eliot's Christian world, we get an astonishingly precise account of what Freud was to call free-association, and that became the Golden Rule, the distinctive thing, about his psychoanalytic method. 'The speaker or writer is uttering something which he does not wholly understand – or which he may even misinterpret when the inspiration has departed.' If God is no longer deemed to be in some sense the source of these unwitting words, then what or who is? It is not too extreme to say that Eliot's description of poetic inspiration is at its most minimal an account of what happens to the patient when he free-associates in analysis; and may, from a certain psychoanalytic point of view, be simply an account of what happens when we speak and write. We never wholly understand our words, we never wholly understand the word understand; and we are never in a position to authoritatively interpret them. Because of the unconscious, one could say crudely, we never quite know what we are on about. And it is perhaps incidentally of interest that Freud claimed to have got his idea of free-association as a therapeutic method from one of the favourite authors of his youth, Ludwig Borne. In 1823 Borne had written an essay entitled 'The Art of Becoming an Original Writer in Three Days', in which he wrote:

Take a few sheets of paper and for three days in succession write down, without any falsification or hypocrisy, everything that comes into your head. Write what you think of yourself, of your women, of the Turkish War, of Goethe ... of the Last Judgement, of those senior to you in authority – and when the three days are over you will be amazed at what novel and startling thoughts have welled up in you. That is the art of becoming an original writer in three days.

Borne's list of what comes into one's mind is in itself revealing; free association is always a period piece. This is the democratisation of inspiration; inspiration and origin-ality for everyone. From inspiration to free-association as the route to, or the sign of originality (for Freud, what is original about oneself is one's history: which is not entirely to one's credit). Not trying to understand what you are writing – indeed, not being able to understand what you are writing – as the way to write. The way to speak is not to choose (or over-choose) your words.

The method of free-association is about what happens when people don't try to understand each other; or rather, when understanding is deferred. If, as Borne suggests, you write down 'without any falsification or hypocrisy, everything that comes into your head,' you are simply following wherever your words take you. And the implication is that this is something we do not usually do, indeed that we might work quite hard to avoid doing. As though to follow our words wherever they may go is surprisingly dangerous. And that the ordinary act of trying to understand what we are saying – the wish for discernible meaning – may be a kind of anxious vigilance. That – at least sometimes – we interrupt ourselves with what we call understanding. So when Eliot writes, appropriately in *Notes Towards the Definition of Culture*, 'It is human, when we do not understand another human being, and cannot ignore him, to exert an unconscious pressure on that person to turn him into something we *can* understand,' and that 'the effect on the person so influenced is liable to be the repression and distortion, rather than the improvement, of the personality,' we cannot help but wonder what we fear will happen if we do not exert this pressure. What else might we do with someone – and the someone who is ourselves – that we cannot understand and cannot ignore? If we lost faith, or even interest in the understanding project, what else might we do with each other? Though Freud never quite goes this far, he does invent a form of therapy that might be described as an interim measure. He says, in effect, if you as the analyst listen to another person and suspend your will to understanding; and if you as the patient defer your appetite for understanding and just let yourself speak, something else will come through in your words. And sometimes it will even seem as if something else – something quite other – is speaking through you.

And this, of course, has consequences for what used to be called the moral life. When Eliot writes, in his great essay on Beaudelaire of 1930, that 'so far as we are human, what we do must be either good or evil,' we may or may not agree, and yet still wonder how we go about making such decisions, how we know just how to assess our actions. It is one thing to say that our actions are either good or evil, it is quite another to be jumping to conclusions about which is which. In the project of suspending internal censorship and saying what comes into one's mind, Freud is encouraging us to play for time, morally. He is not saying our words are not good or evil, he is saying that when we speak we censor ourselves too knowingly. It is as if we live as though there is something inside us – call it a figure, or a voice – who already knows the difference between good and evil, and intervenes accordingly. That we are moralists wanting to be, and fearing to become, more morally complex and subtle. What happens, Freud asks, what do you find yourself saying if you hold on to not understanding, if you hold at bay all your forms of moral judgement that are ordinarily called understanding? Is the idea of Original Sin, for example – or even Freud's idea of a death instinct, some unavoidable internal badness – something that turns up when understanding can no longer be deferred; when it is intolerable not to seem to know what is happening?

I want to suggest that if we de-Christianise Eliot's definition of inspiration – if we take it out of the context that most interests him – it becomes something akin to an alternative to Original Sin. Or, to put it the other way round – to put it perhaps the Freudian way round – a sense of sinfulness could be seen as a pre-emptive strike against inspiration; against 'the speaker or writer uttering something which he does not wholly understand'. That sin, in short, can be used as a form of understanding; part of the unconscious pressure we put on our experience to make it bearable. The idea of sin tells us beforehand that there is such a thing as sin: it settles an issue.

III

Thought asks too much and words tell too much;
because to ask anything is to ask everything, and to
say anything is to ask more.
R. P. Blackmur, *Henry Adams*

What Freud and Eliot are saying, in their different ways, is that the pressures we live under seem to put pressure on us to make them intelligible. That to be human in the best sense is to have some understanding – to be able to give some kind of account – of what we are suffering from. Whether the appeal is made to Original Sin, or personal history and unconscious impersonal instinct, these are gestures towards an understanding of something, and of an acknowledgement of the limits or of the constraints upon such understanding as we have. And yet both Eliot's account of inspiration and Freud's therapeutic Golden Rule of free-association point us in two directions at once. At their most reassuring they tell us that not wholly understanding what we utter – in psychoanalytic terms, deferring one's concern to make sense of oneself – can lead us, in the fullness of time, to a deeper understanding, to a more profound apprehension of what is ultimately only a concealed intelligibility. Sense-making, in other words, is not abrogated as a project, it's just that a more illuminating way of making sense has been found. You have to, as Eliot wrote in 'Little Gidding', with a different intent, 'put off/ Sense and notion. You are not here to verify,/ Instruct yourself, or inform curiosity/ Or carry report ...'; the next words are, 'You are here to kneel/ Where prayer has been valid', but this is also a meticulous description of what Freud encourages the psychoanalytic patient to do, but with a view to something essentially secular and deemed to be therapeutic. Their intentions (if that is the right word) may be radically at odds with each other, but both Freud and Eliot – whatever they may think about the soul of man under psychoanalysis – have a sense of direction. They may not be able to fulfil their wishes, to meet the obligation of their ambitions, but they have, to put it crudely, aims and objectives. Indeed their writings are an attempt to describe the good that they seek.

But there is another direction which they, or their words, point out – even if to call it a direction is in itself misleading. And this is the possibility that through inspiration or free-association, understanding will never emerge; or rather, that what is revealed in inspiration or free-association doesn't so much challenge or stimulate our sense-making capacities as baffle them, or endlessly defer them. That all we can do is interrupt a bewildering delirium. The more outlandish implication is that Eliot's inspired poet, like Freud's free-associating patient, has injected something irreducibly enigmatic into the culture, something no one quite knows what to do with. These irruptions might get assimilated, they seem to suggest, but we need to be mindful what is at stake in the act of assimilation. What Eliot called the 'unconscious pressure on that person to turn him into something we can understand' – which could be redescribed as our consoling myth of interpretation – was understood by him to be, in all likelihood, a distortion and a repression. But what else are we supposed to, what else can we do, with whatever compels our attention, but eludes our grasp?

Eliot's inspired 'speaker or writer' (it is worth noting that it is both), and Freud's ideal patient who has agreed to set aside all his misgivings about what he has to say, have been released in some way from the need to be intelligible to themselves. The pressure to turn themselves into something someone can understand is off, at least for the time being. It is assumed by both writers that the pressure to make sense – to be recognisable as something other than enigmatic – is considerable; that we live under the tyranny of not being too puzzling, both to ourselves and others (it was surrealism that programmatically exploited the irony of assuming that there was less dream-work in the interpretation of the dream than in the dream itself). But above all it is when the pressure to understand is taken off that the most valuable words are spoken or written; the act, the struggle to make oneself intelligible must therefore be some kind of distraction; in psychoanalytic terms, some kind of defence. The words that matter most are the words we don't understand. If previously we have believed that words can only matter when we, at least to some extent, understand them, in what way might they matter to us when we don't? We are, after all, rightly wary of the cultivation of mystery, of the curators of secrecy.

What Eliot took to be characteristic of the soul of man under psychoanalysis – 'the material is so clearly defined ... there is no possibility of tapping the atmosphere of unknown terror and mystery in which our life is passed' – was that this soul was too knowingly organised; it was clearly defined; the rules or principles governing this particular soul's behaviour were, by definition, intelligible. And it's worth noting that his alternative to this is a novel in which this atmosphere of unknown terror and mystery is 'tapped'; not known, or explained, or assimilated, but presented as such. So on at least one of its versions – and I think Eliot is right about this – psychoanalysis is too rational an account of irrationality. It displaces that atmosphere of unknown terror and mystery that is so precious to Eliot. If for Eliot the soul of man under socialism is unrealistically reasonable – social engineering as a cure for original sin; by the same token, the soul of man under psychoanalysis – paradoxically, one might think – is too sure of itself, too complacent about its own descriptions. It puts human authority where, in Eliot's view, there is something else. And this something else – this other source – we may remember, he found in the novels of Dostoyevsky and D. H. Lawrence.

My paraphrase of Eliot's remarks is: people who are psychoanalytically informed – people who have been convinced (if not converted) by Freudian explanations – are likely to understand things in a certain way, are likely to phrase their accounts in a particular language. They will bring a kind of confident assurance to whatever it is they find to be enigmatic; and when this kind of conviction turns up in fiction it will make the fiction too knowing. It will be as though the language in which the fiction is written has fixed referents. Whereas the only conviction a Christian writer will bring to his work will be a conviction of mystery. As Augustine says in one of his sermons, 'Since it is God we are speaking of, you do not understand it. If you could understand it it would not be God.' So the question in secular terms is – and this would be a preposterous, presumptuous question to the Christian believer – how will our lives be better if we entrust ourselves to mystery, rather than to intelligibility, to understanding? God is presumably not a mystery to himself; so if God works in mysterious ways, at least God is there running his mystery. Someone, as it were, knows what's going on, even if, by definition, we can't be party to this knowledge.

If we were to put this in psychoanalytic terms, to redescribe this crudely, we might be asking, is it better to believe in your mother, or to understand her? And the answer would be, you only begin to do what we call understand your mother when your belief in her has been shaken (as it must be). Or we might be asking: should we simply abide by the incest taboo, or should we be enquiring into it, enhancing our understanding of it so we might have a different apprehension of it? And the answer would be, in this case I think, merely another question: how does one go about being curious about the forbidden? From a psycho-analytic point of view, in other words, it is trauma that turns belief (or obedience, or faith) into a need for understanding. Or at least into a need for what William Empson called 'truth-feelings'. Both Freud and Eliot are trying to work out, in their different ways, where understanding comes in. And of course, like everyone else, neither Freud nor Eliot had fixed, formulated beliefs about the nature of understanding; their views evolved. But staging them – if not framing them – as antagonists allows us to review our options. Freud can be too narrowly knowing, too rhetorically persuasive in his explanations and in his belief in the value of understanding our lives (understanding our lives, that is, in the psycho-analytic way). Eliot, as a Christian, can perhaps be too knowing in his distrust of explanations, in his scepticism about our all-too-human accounts.

Both Freud and Eliot, of course, appeal to non-human forms of authority to make the human world intelligible. For

Eliot there is the mystery of God, and the curse of Original Sin, 'the atmosphere of unknown terror and mystery in which our life is passed, and which psychoanalysis has not yet analysed'. For Freud there is instinctual life (the drives) and incest. The soul of man under psychoanalysis – and the phrase itself is odd because, even though Freud uses the word soul, it is not obvious what a psychoanalytic soul would be like – is a transgressive soul. What Freudian man and woman want is not to be saved, but to satisfy their forbidden desire. Which means to put their lives in mortal danger. For Eliot, for Eliot's Christian, there is, one might say, a destination, even if it is not within a person's gift to secure it; for Freud, for Freudian souls, it is not clear whether there is a destination or only a direction.

IV

... what is meant by defending one's goods is one and the same thing as forbidding oneself from enjoying them.
Jacques Lacan, *The Ethics of Psychoanalysis*

Eliot, as Christopher Ricks among others has shown, was always shrewdly allusive; so it is perhaps worth wondering, by way of conclusion, why he might have yoked Wilde and Freud together – and indeed psychoanalysis and socialism – in his throwaway phrase 'the soul of man under psycho-analysis'. Wilde's famous essay of 1891 does not in any obvious way bear any kind of family resemblance to the psychoanalytic writing Eliot was referring to. There is, in *The Soul of Man under Socialism*, a radical critique of altruism and a paganising of Christ; 'What Jesus meant was this,' Wilde writes, 'He said to man, ''you have a wonderful personality. Develop it. Be yourself." ' This, of course, would not be Eliot's version of Christ, this would be Eliot's version of play-acting with religion ('Disobedience', Wilde writes, '. . . is man's original virtue'). Nor would the young Eliot have been overly impressed by Wilde's ceding of all authority to the individual; 'The true artist', Wilde writes, 'is a man who believes absolutely in himself, because he is absolutely himself.' 'All authority', Wilde writes, 'is quite degrading. It degrades those who exercise it, and degrades those over whom it is exercised.'

Wilde's promotion of the flagrantly self-invented individual – his new religion of Individualism – might, one imagines, have amused Freud (and even interested him); but the soul of man under psychoanalysis – the individual as Freud decribed him – was more driven than self-fashioned, more riven than whole; had indeed dispensed with the whole notion of what Wilde calls 'perfect harmony'. Man may have, as Wilde says, 'sought to live intensely, fully, perfectly', but, Freud adds, he is too frightened of his own nature, of his own desire to do so. What man seeks, Freud says, is not the Sovereign Good of traditional moral philosophy; nor indeed of God's love, or grace, or redemption. What man (as Freud still calls us) seeks is the forbidden object of incestuous desire. We seek, that is to say, a pleasure we cannot bear, not a moral or religious ideal that, were we to achieve it, would complete us. And because what we desire is forbidden – because we as it were recognise the object of desire in our sense of mortal risk – we need to obscure it, to conceal it from ourselves. In brief, Wilde's proposed new individual under socialism is – from both Freud and Eliot's point of view – too jaunty in his freedom. He really seems to believe that his life is his own, and if he is sufficiently gifted he can make of it what he will. He is a man on his own terms. His descriptions of himself can be referred to no higher or lower authority. Answerable to no one else, he is to his own taste (or he is nothing).

And yet despite all this Eliot, as usual, has picked something up, has heard something in psychoanalysis that even psychoanalysts themselves may not have wanted to hear. 'Happiness', Freud wrote in *Civilisation and its Discontents*, 'is something entirely subjective.' Not only is our pleasure idiosyncratic, it is revealing of our idiosyncrasy. If you want to find out who you are, recognise what makes you happy. Your subjectivity, Freud suggests, is in your happiness. Freud, in other words, is not saying – to adapt Tolstoy's infamous beginning – that all happy individuals are the same. In connecting the soul of man under psychoanalysis with *The Soul of Man under* (Wilde's) *Socialism*, Eliot was, I think, locating something that troubled him, and that Freud and Wilde were preoccupied by. And this was the possibility that the individual realises himself – reveals himself – through his pleasure. 'It is', Wilde writes, 'mentally and morally injurious to man to do anything in which he does not find pleasure.' Wilde is quite clear – or rather, quite insistent – in his essay that suffering is bad for us.

The Christ of medieval Christianity was, Wilde writes, 'realising his perfection through pain ... The injustice of men is great. It was necessary that pain should be put forward as a mode of self-realisation.' But, Wilde writes, this is all wrong; this is utterly misleading; 'pain is not the ultimate mode of perfection. It is merely provisional, and a protest ... Pleasure is Nature's test, her sign of approval.' Suffering as a fascination, as a vocation, is just what Wilde wants to provoke us out of. It is not our suffering we need to understand, it is our happiness; we need only understand our pain so we can get to our pleasure. Pain is a 'protest' against the absence of pleasure. Like Freud, Wilde has no truck with sin; it is through pleasure that what he calls 'Individualism' becomes possible. The aim, in his view, of both socialism and science is 'Individualism expressing itself through joy'; and the artist is the exemplary individualist. 'Art is individualism', Wilde writes, 'and individualism is a disturbing and disintegrating force'; and if the artist 'does not do it [art] solely for his own pleasure, he is not an artist at all'. This is not, of course, worlds apart from the view Freud was to take thirteen years later in his paper 'Creative Writers and Daydreaming' (1908), in which Freud celebrates, indeed privileges the artist because he is a more tenacious hedonist than what Freud calls the ordinary person. For Freud, as for Wilde in *The Soul of Man under Socialism*, what is to be understood, what is to be sponsored, is how modern people – as 'clever animals' – safeguard and sustain their pleasure-seeking; and how it is that this pleasure-seeking is their lifeline to everything that matters in life.

Wilde's writing was a problem to Eliot – and particularly perhaps Wilde's writing in *The Soul of Man under Socialism* – because it is an experiment in making no appeal to a non-human authority. You can neither, as it were, ask God why you are unhappy; nor can you start explaining and understanding your unhappiness by telling a story about human nature and its instinctual vicissitudes. Wilde says, in effect: we have nothing but our own ingenuity (which we might call wit), and it doesn't much matter where, if anywhere, it comes from. For Eliot this would be play-acting as though one was writing the play oneself; for Freud it would be the apotheosis of egotism, of the ego's illusion of autonomy. For both Freud and Eliot it is a question of where you locate, how you describe, the non-human authority which, in their view, we cannot help but abide by. For Eliot, there was what his biographer Lyndall Gordon called 'a consuming search for salvation'; for Freud, there was no salvation, no redemptive myth, but the secular alternative: a realistic apprehension of one's nature.

The soul of man under psychoanalysis wants, knows what he wants, and doesn't want to know that he knows what he wants. As Eliot intimates, we could live under psychoanalysis in the way we might experience ourselves as living under socialism; that is, under an imposed regime of descriptions of what we want, what we like, and what we are like. And we may feel similarly oppressed living under psychoanalysis as we might if we were ever to live under socialism. Eliot's distaste for both systems is resonant in his phrasing of the question. Yet Freud and Wilde and Eliot would all agree that we are inherently transgressive creatures; for Wilde this is the point, for Eliot this is the problem, and for Freud it is the point and the problem. And this is why – if there is a soul, and if it has to be under anything – I prefer the soul of men and women under psychoanalysis. Because psychoanalysis tells us a story about ourselves that both consoles and confounds us. It gives us a myth and a mystery, a coherent narrative and a disturbing incoherence simultaneously; at one fell swoop our lives seem to make perfect sense, and are perfectly senseless.

Psychoanalysis can tell us a reassuringly normative story; we begin by desiring (and wanting to murder) the parents; registering the horror, not to mention the impossibility of this project, we more or less relinquish it. We renounce our first desires and wait; and eventually, if all goes well, we will as adults find people who are sufficiently reminiscent of the parents to be exciting, but sufficiently different so we can consummate our desire. We want something; we realise the dangerous error of our ways; and we find the substitutes that can satisfy us. We can, in a sense, have what we want because it isn't what we really want, which we could never have anyway. This is a story about human development as both possible and potentially satisfying. Good-enough mothers and fathers facilitating good-enough lives for their children.

But then there is the parallel text to this story – the other life that makes our lives double – and that is more akin to Eliot's atmosphere of mystery and terror. In this life our desire is ineluctably, undistractedly, transgressive; in this life we are driven to always approach and avoid the objects of desire, and what makes us feel most alive makes us feel we are risking our lives. In this life the good-enough mother is always a bad-enough tantalisation. In this life uncanniness is way in excess of our canniness; our actions feel at once inevitable and unintelligible (and so as shorthand we say we are in love, or we are tragic heroes, or we have made a Freudian slip). We do not know what we are doing, and yet we feel ineluctably involved in our lives. Where once there were security operations, now there is risk; where once safety was the be-all and end-all, now fear is preferred. A sense of aliveness displaces a sense of certainty as a paramount consideration. Surprise and dread are the order of the day. In our transgressive life it is as though there is something – or someone – we seem to value more than our lives, more than life itself.

'Life is impoverished,' Freud wrote in 1915, 'it loses in interest, when the highest stake in the game of living, life itself, may not be risked.' The essay from which this comes is entitled 'Thoughts for the Times on War and Death'; but the analogy Freud uses to illustrate his point makes a comparison with relations between the sexes. Life, he writes, 'becomes as shallow and empty as, let us say, an American flirtation, in which it is understood from the first that nothing is to happen, as contrasted with a Continental love affair in which both partners must constantly bear its serious consequences in mind.' The soul of man under psychoanalysis is about nothing more and nothing less than the relation between the sexes, about what it is to live with nothing to love and hate but each other. For the soul of man under psychoanalysis the 'atmosphere of unknown terror and mystery' emanates from nowhere but ourselves. And all we can go on doing is describing what it is like, in all its unlikeness.

The Strange, the Weird
and the Uncanny

Dream in which waking life begins to play a role.
Nietzsche, unpublished writings, spring–summer 1874

Of these words we use for the quotidian sublime – for whatever is bizarre and disturbing in everyday life, for the enigmas that ruffle our routines – uncanny is, as it were, the strangest. People can be strange and weird, but only experiences are uncanny. And yet people are canny in a way we don't think of experiences as being. The whole notion of oddity reassures us that there is plenty of familiarity around, but the uncanny doesn't seem to be the exception that proves the rule. Canniness can't help us with the uncanny, because it's something else altogether.

Freud – or rather, his translator James Strachey – tried to make it part of the jargon of psychoanalysis. *Unheimlich* (unhomely) became 'the Uncanny', and the Uncanny was the strangeness of the all-too-familiar. The shock of the old staged as, appearing to be, the shock of the new. In Freud's view an uncanny experience was a memory – an encounter in which, unbeknown to ourselves, the present collapsed back into the past – in which the forbidden announced itself again. Freud quotes Schelling's description of the uncanny as whatever 'ought to have remained secret and concealed, but which has come to light'. Unacceptable desires are secrets waiting, looking for an opportunity to expose themselves. And the implication is that these desires are not really strange to us, but that we have needed, for safety's sake, to estrange ourselves from them. It is like treating members of one's family as though they were unwelcome guests, or foreign bodies. The uncanny reminds us that everything is too close to home. One's deepest wish is that there is no place like home, because one's deepest fear is that there is no place unlike home. And home is where the trouble starts.

And yet we may wonder now what hope there is for the strange, the weird or the uncanny if we think we know what these words are referring to. Our language for that which we have not ourselves invented, and cannot arrange, is bound to be ironic – partly, of course, because language itself is something we have invented (unlike a lot of other things in the world). How strange, weird or uncanny can God, the Devil or incest be? Compared, say, with luck, coincidence or affinity? Strange, weird and uncanny, that is to say, are words peculiarly undone by definition. If they say what they mean, what could they possibly mean? Dictionaries can only diminish them, and usage can never be unknowing enough. As words they may be more like gasps or exclamations. It is as though these are the words that have to be taken on their own terms, or as their own terms. Words to refer to things that words can't refer to; words that refer to other words, but only disingenuously. It is very difficult for us to believe that the unaccountable doesn't make us accountable to somebody, or something. Faced with such strangeness as occurs – and perhaps our dreams are as good an emblem of this as anything – we are likely to problem-solve (provide explanations), acknowledge mystery, or make offerings to gods. We are not, in other words, inclined to take strangeness for granted.

Freud's domesticating of the Uncanny – his making it, like

everything else, a family affair – is an example of precisely the thing he describes. That by normalising our experience – by living as though we are more or less familiar to ourselves, in a more or less familiar world – our lives become more disturbing (and disturbed) rather than less. There is nothing more provocative than a routine, no surprises without expectations, great or small. As long as we go on believing in repetition, words like weird and strange will go on seeming to make sense to us. They will go on referring us back to the patterns they disrupt, to the reassurances they unsettle. But it would be canny now not to be thinking always (or only) in these terms. To live as if what we call the uncanny is uncalculated and uncalculating.

On What We Need

Actions and motives must be instances of types, kinds, generalities, if they are to be understood, and their being such types is some sort of function of participants who acknowledge, are committed to, there being such types.

Robert B. Pippin, *Henry James and Modern Moral Life*

The best thing psychoanalysts do is clinical work. But the second best thing they do that is not unrelated to this work is to come up with descriptions of what they believe people need. That is, need in order to live what they consider good-enough lives. This is usually referred to as psychoanalytic theory, but the basic structure – the argument, as it were, and it is always an argument – is quite simple. A need or a set of needs is posited – more or less proven if the theorist is scientifically minded, more or less eloquently asserted if she is not – and more or less adequate responses to these needs are then described. The needs have consequences, as do the responses to them. If to call an inclination a need is a rhetorical way of stressing its importance – at one end of this imaginary spectrum we have needs, at the other end we have whims or fashions, say – then psychoanalysis can be seen as adding to the cultural-description pool accounts of who we are in terms of what we need. In the need-narrative a

118

need is something that, should it go unmet, disfigures the person bearing it. There is, that is to say, nothing more essential to, or about a person than his needs.

But in a time, like all times, critical of previous essentialisms; and, unlike all times, critical of the whole notion of essences, needs become a kind of test case. People's needs, like their instincts, are up for grabs. Any of us might be able to come up with a new need, or alternatively might start working out the consequences of doing without words like need (or instinct, or passion, or any of the other old-world nicknames that we and God used about us). And even when we thought we could at least settle for a base-line of eating and breathing (with sex as an optional extra), psychoanalysis showed us that there is no registered need that is not exploitable, no officially sanctioned need that is not adaptable to alternative uses and pleasures. We may need to eat and breathe in order to live, but we may not need to live. If we are, as most versions of psychoanalysis agree, divided against ourselves, in conflict, then our so-called needs become just as precarious, just as puzzling, as any other of our wished-for essentialisms. Instead of stating what people need it might be more revealing to say something like: if we agree to decide that people need X, then these are the consequences we can imagine; and we can find out more of the consequences by hearing from people who live as if this need is true (so-called perversions are not a problem for people, but their consequences can be). What we think of as our needs are intimately bound up with what we think of as our options, our opportunities, and our ideals. 'The value of our ideals', John Dewey wrote in *Art as Experience*, 'lies in the experiences to which they lead.' And the same is true of the value of what we are moved to call our needs. Because what we call our needs lead us into certain kinds of experiences, it matters what we call our needs (those who think of attachment as a need, for example, don't seem to have much to tell us about ecstacy; those who promote self-knowledge distract us from the thrills of self-anonymity). To say something is a need is to say – or to want to say – that there is no way round it. And to say something is a need from a psychoanalytic point of view is to say that for every need, we are likely also to need to believe that we can find a way round it.

I want to give an account of what Emmanuel Ghent thinks we need, and of how needing works; which includes, of course, an account of how it can go wrong. I want to say what Ghent thinks we need – in his words as far as possible, which means in my words too – and then try to answer the thornier question of why I think we should value the things that Ghent, in his writing, is persuading us to take seriously. I want to think, in other words, about the experiences to which his ideals might lead. And I want to read him backwards – in reverse chronological order – so that his remarkable writing unravels rather than seeming to progress; to accumulate retroactively is, after all, the psychoanalytic way. If we believe in deferred action, if we believe in dream-work, even if we believe in development – or growth, as Ghent is also prone to call it – we can only read backwards. Or rather, reading backwards is the best way of seeing how things have turned out; and how long things can take to say what they mean to us.

Just before we start working backwards I think we need to bear in mind, as a kind of epigraph, one of the credos mentioned in passing in Ghent's Credo: 'The Dialectics of One-Person and Two-Person Psychologies'. 'It became clear', he writes, 'that whatever I might say about what I believe, can at best only be true at this moment.' This is at once a truthful and a disarming remark. It acknowledges that we cannot be held to our beliefs, that to foist a consistency upon ourselves is to freeze time; to hold something back by holding something over. But if what he says about what he believes 'can at best only be true at this moment', when was that? It seems to me right that the truth is in the moment, and that what we can say about what we believe is always of the moment. And that our beliefs, such as they are, are only what we can say about them. I want to make a meal of this for two reasons. Firstly because I think Ghent writes a psychoanalysis of the proliferating self in which what we might refer to as truths or beliefs are momentary bulletins from a continually evolving project. That in the to-and-fro between development and arrested development the medium is the unstoppable time of a life (the monumental longings of theory give way to the needs, the fashionings of the moment). That, in short, Ghent's psychoanalysis is committed to transformations and not resolutions, not so much to the exploration of states of mind, but to the sense that states of mind are themselves exploratory. We are always seeking out our possibilities even, or especially, when we are most deadlocked. What he refers to as 'yielding the defensive superstructure, being known, found, penetrated, recognised', are all break-outs and breakthroughs. Yielding is letting something happen, to let something happen. And it assumes that we have been somehow unyielding, and that we would be better off living as if there were things worth yielding to.

But secondly, and perhaps less obviously, Ghent's credo about momentariness – about the momentary truth of his believings – is also a more oblique allusion to something that Ghent has been quite explicitly exercised by throughout his writing: and that is the nature of need. If we were crudish Freudians we might say a belief is the sublimation of a need; or beliefs are reaction-formations against needs. Whether we think of our beliefs as informed by our needs, or disguised statements about need, from a psychoanalytic point of view needs and beliefs are linked, if not actually inextricable. If we rewrite Ghent's sentence – replace belief with need – it reads as follows. 'It became clear that whatever I might say about what I need, can at best only be true at this moment.' That seems to me to be a radical innovation in psychoanalytic thinking, and is of a piece with what Ghent has been working on and working out about need. That needs, like beliefs, are not essences that are fixed, but develop inside a person; they are not a pre-arranged repertoire or a set of Platonic forms, but are essentially circumstantial, inclinations of the moment and the context; and therefore needs have no known essence. They are not urgencies waiting to happen, personal imperatives ready to go off, but artefacts made in relationship. Needs are more like personal experiments in living than designs for a life. The novelist E. M. Forster famously said, 'How can I know what I think until I see what I say?' Ghent says, 'how can I know what I need until someone responds to something I do?' I do something, either knowingly or unwittingly; someone responds in a way that might seem simply right, or at once apt and surprising, and then I realise, in retrospect, that what I had been doing was needing. I had been, as it were, caught in the act. I had wanted something without knowing what I wanted, or even, perhaps, that I was wanting.

There is, in other words, to adapt Winnicott's formula, no such thing as a need, there is always a need and its correspondent. We are full of indeterminate possibilities, Ghent implies, that require suitable recognition in order to make us start talking about them as needs. They are not so much inbuilt projects to be exercised or thwarted; they are rather reconstructed after the transformative event of a sign being read or acted on in a certain way. As we shall see, what Ghent calls neediness is the baffling of this experience. From this point of view, dependence is not on another person to gratify our needs, but to create them through their response. So what Ghent adds to the more familiar psycho-analytic story about needing in development is the extraordinary and paradoxical idea that a need is something you didn't know you had until someone happened to gratify it, or validate it.

II

Towards real experiences we generally adopt
a uniformly passive attitude and succumb to the
influence of our material environment.
Freud, 'The Uncanny'

There is of course by now a genre of psychoanalytic vignette in which either the analyst or the so-called patient do something, either utterly mundane or a bit out of the ordinary, and it is vividly transformational. Balint's patient did a somersault, Sandler passed a tissue, and Winnicott did many such things making this particular genre of analytic writing his signature tune. The emphasis is usually on doing instead of or as well as saying, so Kleinians and orthodox Freudians and Lacanians don't tend to go in for these plays within the play. In 'Interaction in the Psychoanalytic Situation' (1995), Ghent has an unusually interesting clinical vignette, which is in itself impressive given that it is the point of the genre to make the reader wonder what is being shown here, a new shareable technique, or an astonishingly talented therapist at work? When, in psychoanalytic writing, a transformation scene is offered – and especially when the epiphany is promoted by a gesture – the demand on the reader is perplexing. We may, for example, wonder what we are supposed to do with this. What I think is remarkable about Ghent's vignette is that his gesture is at once unaccountable and straightforward. Claims are not being made for his genius, but for there being something by definition inexplicable in the nature of recognition. Indeed, if it was explicable it wouldn't be what he thinks of as recognition, it would be a species of proselytising. 'Many years ago,' he writes,

I had an office on the ground floor of a Greenwich village brown-stone. As it faced out on a large garden and much open space, the office was quite susceptible to chilly drafts on windy winter days. One such day a woman patient was haltingly recounting, as was her wont, the details of some event that had recently occurred; I cannot now recall the content. She was sitting in a chair at right angles to me, about fifteen feet from the windows. Suddenly, but not abruptly, I got up, went over to where a Scottish throw was folded on the couch, picked it up, covered her lap and legs with it, and returned to my chair. As I sat down I noticed, *to my surprise*, that she was sobbing silently. It was the first time in our work, by then over two years in duration, that there was any indication of distress, pain, or even sadness. After some time, her first words were, 'I didn't even know I was feeling cold', and then she wept profusely. The event was a turning point.

It is characteristic of Ghent that he should then follow this with two further, and similar, accounts from Irwin Hoffman and Darlene Ehrenberg. Clearly something other than a unique clinical sensibility is being spoken up for here. And there are two overall points he wants to make. Firstly that in these examples there is no 'question of demand, the shibboleth of the neediness that often masquerades as need but in actuality is organised as a defense against – a blackwashing of – the need for caring responsiveness'. And secondly that 'the phrase "to my surprise" was part of the therapist's reaction. It is as if the therapist's attention has been claimed by something unexpected, a loud hint that a new vista, a new insight, is brewing.' In other words, the patient has not, to all intents and purposes, asked for anything; and the therapist has been surprised by what he's got to give at that moment. Neither the patient nor the analyst are acting on, or speaking about, their ostensive beliefs.

Ghent's patient didn't know she was feeling cold until he covered her; she could only recognise what she was feeling after he had, however unknowingly, sensed this, and acted on his imagining. It is the kind of thing a parent might do with a young child, such is its touching and wholly convincing ordinariness. It seems to me to be a wonderful piece of writing re-presenting a remarkable moment of therapy. She had expressed her unhappiness, could only do so, *after* Ghent had recognised it and gone some way to meet it. It is virtually true to say that, from her point of view, she had not needed looking after until Ghent had looked after her. At that moment she had not apparently wanted anything; and Ghent had given her something and then was surprised, not by what he had given her, but by her response to it. His ordinary recognition prompts her recognition which surprises him. What had been missing in her – expression of her unhappiness – was made possible when Ghent satisfied her unthought need.

It would be misleading, I think, to say that Ghent's gesture released something in her because that would imply that a something – pain, say – had been pent up in her until that moment. Ghent's account leaves this instructively ambiguous. Perhaps it would be truer and more useful to say that through Ghent's enacted recognition this woman could construct an unhappiness for the first time. Either there had been a need lurking in her all this time; or, at that moment, a need was crystallised. In one sense, the need to be looked after could never be a new need; but it would be a description of this woman's unhappiness to say that she was so unhappy because it felt as if it was a new need. 'Of special moment in each of these examples', Ghent writes, and moment is the word, 'is that along with the old pattern of behaviour, something new was happening.' The repetition – '[she] was haltingly recounting, as was her wont, the details of some event that had recently occurred; I cannot now recall the content' – is 'mixed in', Ghent writes, with another need; and the mixing, as we shall see, is as important as this other need that is 'usually much weaker and less developed; it is an expansive rather than a conservative system; one whose tendency or need is either to seek out a new quality of experience, or to destabilise the smooth functioning of the old, constrictive system.' There is, Ghent is saying, a need for the new; and if it is genuinely new, of course, neither the therapist nor the patient could know beforehand what it might be. And if the need for the new is 'mixed in' – that is, to use another of Ghent's good fusional words, blended, or even inextricable from – then it has to be part of the analyst's skill to see both happening at once; to acknowledge the mix and do a bit of disentangling. The need for the new, I am suggesting, Ghent is suggesting, is also the need for new needs. And when Ghent says in this paper that there is 'a need in the patient for a quality of experience in the analysis without which therapeutic effect will be minimal', he is saying that the patient depends upon the therapist not being too knowing about the patient's needs. To acknowledge the need for new needs is to acknowledge, by definition, not knowing what they are. The so-called repetition compulsion, one might say, stabilises the proliferation of needs.

In a commentary two years previously on a paper by Peter Shabad, Ghent is keen to show what kind of meanings the word need 'has taken on'. Wanting to 'illustrate the range of attitudes about the question of encountering the patient's need', Ghent distinguishes what he calls 'at least two quite different meanings that attach to the word "need"'. The distinction he goes on to make might be described as need looked at from the inside, from the point of view of someone feeling what they call a need; and the view from outside, a kind of cultural consensus about what human beings fundamentally consist of. 'Is need', he asks, 'to be regarded as expressive of a requirement for the healthy welfare and development of the person, or should it be employed on the basis of the feeling of need, its urgency, peremptoriness, demand?' This seems to me to be a rather interesting way of putting it; because it pits my freedom as a patient to define anything felt as urgent, peremptory or demanding in myself as a need – and therefore as something to which I am entitled – against the analyst, as expert on human nature, who knows beforehand what the patient is entitled to regard as a need. And this, of course, has consequences for the responding analyst. To put it schematically, the analyst will respond differently to what she might believe is conducive to 'the healthy welfare and development of a person' than she does to the patient's every whim. And yet as Ghent intimates – though I'm not sure he would endorse this – in a pragmatist vein, things may be only the way we describe them. I am free to call anything in myself, any inclination in myself that particularly matters to me, a need. Indeed by describing it as a need, in this culture, I am more likely to get it attended to. If needs, in my culture, tend to be defined by the qualities of urgency, peremptoriness and demand, and needs are given priority over wants, it would be the intelligent policy of, in Nietzsche's phrase, 'a clever animal' to describe his own priorities as needs. This is what language – which makes us in a sense the cleverest animals – is for: to persuade people. In the clash and collaboration of the patient's and the analyst's rhetorics, the drama of who has got the best line on need is enacted.

But in order to make a good case for a better life, it is useful to distinguish, as Ghent does, between qualities of need; between, as he calls it in his language, need and neediness. For me, Ghent has the best line going in psychoanalytic writing on need. Though in asserting this I have nothing to offer by way of justification except my unwilled agreement – the affinity and assent induced by his writing – and my knowledge that more knowledge about myself wouldn't give me any better grounds for valuing what he has been keen to say. Ghent proposes that we should distinguish

between appropriate and legitimate need and neediness. By legitimate needs I include the needs for recognition and affirmation – to be treated with empathic responsiveness, to be understood – as well as the need to use the object, the expression of which may present substantial difficulty for the analyst in that it is likely to spill over into object abuse.

Because of this spillage – because of the blending and mixing of these apparently contradictory projects – Ghent's distinction allows both the patient and the analyst a remarkable margin of freedom in the analytic encounter. Because it must be part of the legitimate need for recognition and affirmation that the patient could be recognised and affirmed as somebody who, for good reason, might want to call any urgency in himself a need. Paradoxically, in distinguishing need and neediness, Ghent legitimates the value of both. It may be one of my needs to perform my neediness. Neediness, one might say, is the best form the patient has found for his needs so far. So as we go backwards with Ghent we go from need and neediness, through paradox and process, to masochism, submission and surrender. Prospectively, of course, this project had no inevitability to it; retrospectively it can be construed as a remarkably inspired and persistent account of something that by his standards – and there is no attitudinising in Ghent's writing – was strongly stated in 1994: 'I find it distressing when I encounter Procrusteanism in any form.' Just as there is no attitudinising in Ghent's work there is also remarkably little mythology. Procrusteanism is a well-known analytic approach. Procrustes, in the words of Lempriere, 'was a famous robber of Attica ... He tied travellers on a bed, and, if their length exceeded that of the bed, cut off part of their limbs to make their length equal to that of the bed; but if they were shorter he stretched their bodies till they were of the same length.' What Ghent calls Procrusteanism in any form – which is itself amusing and amused, as Procrusteanism is about keeping forms down to a minimum – is about cutting people down to size and making them fit. Ghent has embarked on a peculiarly and paradoxically difficult task: to find an alternative, in psycho-analysis, to Procrusteanism; the possibility that in the theory and practice of psychoanalysis there may be something on offer other than the Procrusteanism of everyday life.

III

*That sense of strain resolved, of a floating energy
against the stream ...*
Barbara Everett, 'Donne and Secrecy'

If Ghent is often asking, one way or another, is there
anything else in so-called perversion other than perversion?
then the image of Procrustes, tailoring his victims to his bed,
is telling in its sexual starkness. It is at once a story about
what theories and theorists can do to themselves and others,
and what people can do to themselves and others. It is an
image of how people can disfigure each other for what
seems like the sake of convenience. Procrustes is, rather too
literally, persuading the bodies of his victims to fit the bed. It
is, in other words, another transformation scene, a malign
one. So it is not incidental, I think, for Ghent to have
included Procrustes in passing; and nor is it unrelated that
there are two pieces of psychoanalytic writing that Ghent
quotes more than once that are about this essential matter of
how people go about changing each other – what Ghent
calls 'the larger question of what makes for personality
change and emotional growth'. Because Ghent quotes other
people so well – which is itself an exemplary instance of the
use of an object – it is striking when such an uninsistent
writer keeps going back to something. We must all have
passages of psychoanalytic writing that we are keen to
quote, or re-read, or determinedly avoid quoting; passages
which elicit a strong transference because they reveal
simultaneously an affinity and a dilemma that is close to
our hearts. There are two passages that recur in Ghent's
writing, one famous one from Winnicott and one no less
intriguing from Arnold Cooper. And, perhaps unsurpris-

ingly, they are linked. They are both questions from Procrustes' bed. From Cooper's paper, entitled 'Psychic Change: Development in the theory of psychoanalytic techniques' (1992), Ghent quotes him as saying:

It is less than clear that cognitive aspects of insight are essential for psychic change ... Stanley Greenspan ... has shown that better mothering or removal from an abusive situation produces power-ful and lasting changes in the child, even though the child is not helped to develop insight into what is going on ... This also brings up the question of non-analytic change, and the importance for analysis of our better understanding of conversion experiences – whether St Paul or Malcom X – and the importance of peak affect.

What Cooper is referring to might be thought of as a triangle of alternatives for transformation: a change of external environment, the revelation leading to conversion, or changing the internal environment through insight. The psychoanalytic position, Cooper intimates, is uneasily poised between the latter two. The patient does, of course, change his external environment by going into the analyst's consulting room; and in so far as the analyst and her patient share a language, something akin to a conversion experience might have gone on. Or to put it another way, if analysts don't describe themselves as being converted to psycho-analysis how would they rather put it? In the same way that Ghent's work looks for an alternative to the so-called perverse solution of sado-masochism, it is to alternatives to conversion that he pays attention. Cooper's suggestion of the importance, for psychoanalysis, of what he calls 'non-analytic change' also links up with the tactful and rather understated references in Ghent's writing to meditation.

The quotation from Winnicott's 1969 paper, 'The Use of an Object and Relating through Identifications', is equally evidently at the heart of Ghent's preoccupations. In what

Ghent calls 'an almost diagrammatic example', he quotes Winnicott saying:

Two babies are feeding at the breast; one is feeding on the self in the form of projections, and the other is feeding on [using] milk from a woman's breast ... The change does not come about automatically, by maturational process alone ... Mothers, like analysts, can be good or not good enough; some can and some cannot carry the baby over from relating to usage. [This transition] is the most difficult thing, perhaps, in human development ... and the most irksome of all the early failures that come for mending ... the change (from relating to use) means that the subject destroys the object (as subjective object) and the object, if it survives destruction, is now real.

All psychoanalytic writers write about change; but the stronger theorists – or rather, the theorists who tend to attract more of our attention – tend, either explicitly or implicitly, to tell us the difference between good change and bad change. They specify, in other words, the direction in which change should take place. Lacan says that bad change for the patient is the illusion of an improved adaptation to the environment or a greater mastery over the self; good change, Klein says, is entering into the depressive position. Good change, Winnicott says here, is what the self can become in the process of making the object real. What Cooper raises more openly – and I think this might be part of his appeal for Ghent – is not merely the question of how good change might be effected, but the thornier question of what it is that makes us think of any particular kind of change as good. Winnicott's rhetoric of true selves and real objects, for example, lures us away from the more vulgar questions like what's the big deal about relating to a so-called real object? Why is that self-evidently a good life project, indeed such an essential life project that, in

Winnicott's words, inability to achieve this is a 'failure that comes for mending'? Of course, <u>we could all give a good answer to these questions, but the answers won't rescue us from the predicament</u> – which I think Ghent's work has always been looking at – <u>that no story about change is exempt from a whole range of prior judgements about what we consider, more or less tacitly, a good life</u>. When we say it is bad for adolescents to take drugs, or good for adults to become parents, there is always a trawl of values in the wake of these statements. When Ghent, who in the early sixties wrote a paper on scarcity, invites us to put our money on paradox and surrender, on acceptance as opposed to resignation, on what Cooper calls 'non-analytic' forms of change as well as, or complementary to, psychoanalysis, he is both asserting his own sense of value, but also persuading us to value the kinds of experience in which we might be able to find out just what it is we do value, however momentarily.

What Ghent calls paradox and surrender – which are, as we shall see, related phenomena – I would also want to call experiments in personal morality. In entertaining a paradox we are free of mutually exclusive options; in surrendering to an experience, in Ghent's version, we abrogate our previous sense of what our possibilities are. Ghent says: the best direction change can take is the direction in which we cannot know where our change will take us. This, to put it mildly, has radical moral and political implications (<u>Ghent</u> is for me an exemplary psychoanalytic writer by being at once plain and straightforward and wonderfully oblique). Just as '<u>Masochism, Submission, Surrender</u>' is the best thing <u>I have ever read about listening to music</u>, though music is <u>not mentioned</u>, by the same token Ghent's writing seems to me ferociously political by being mild-mannered and

← ABOUT LISTENING TO MUSIC

making only the odd glancing reference to something we might think of as politics.

Wittingly or unwittingly, or wittingly and unwittingly, Ghent is an artful writer, and we should take this to heart. And nowhere is this more evident than in what are for me his two finest papers, 'Paradox and Process' (1992) and 'Masochism, Submission, Surrender (1) – Masochism as a Perversion of Surrender' (1990). Everything I have ever come across by Ghent is worth reading, but for me these two papers are inexhaustibly interesting. Having, as he once put it, 'contributed to the cause of slaying the one person dragon', and worried away about the connection, if any, between information and transformation, it is in his account of paradox and surrender that Ghent really starts something off in psychoanalysis, while fairly and squarely acknowledging his debts to certain strands of the psychoanalytic tradition. We don't have to over-value originality – and I imagine that Ghent himself doesn't need to over-value this now over-valued commodity – to notice that these two papers bring to light, in an unusually vivid way, much that has been latent and lurking in the British Independent group, in relational psychoanalysis, and in Kohut, without doing anything as banal and tiresome as making a synthesis. Ghent doesn't bring all this together; he brings out something of his own in bringing them together. I don't want to paraphrase these unsummarisable papers, because they are too good for that. I just want to, by way of conclusion, pick out a few highlights; when Ghent simply tells us what we need in a way that makes us wonder about what we need and how we go about doing this odd thing.

When Ghent wants to talk about paradox he starts talking about need; and this, in a sense, is strange. What, after all, could be less paradoxical than a need? It would seem as though, by definition, something is either a need or it isn't. 'Among the questions to be touched on in this paper,' he writes, one of them is 'How can there be both need and no need at the same time?' It's like the children's joke, when is a door not a door? When it's ajar. Except that Ghent is proposing not a synthesis or a resolution, but that third thing that isn't exactly a third thing, called a paradox. Paradox, Ghent tells us, 'lives in the world of the aesthetic; it points the way to insight without laying an interpretation upon us.' Pointing the way is a direction, but not a prescription; it is the difference between me saying go to London rather than go in the direction of London. If I say go to London, we both know where you are going. Needs, it is intimated, may be more akin to directions than destinations. And so we might say, paradoxically, that needs get distorted when destinations are privileged (the person with a so-called perverse desire knows exactly where he's going). That needing is a process – to use the other term of Ghent's title – and a process that involves a paradox (to lay an interpretation on a process would be unpromising). What Ghent proposes instead is that the thing about need – the point of needing – is that we can't tell the good need from the bad need. If we can tell, then it's not a need.

'How, then, to understand', Ghent asks,

the relation between neediness and need, between 'bad need' and 'good need'? As with most paradoxical and ambiguous situations, our intellect and our scientific imagination wish to choose between alternatives, to come down on one or the other side. It is either this or that. But in real life we are often in an intermediate zone, where ambiguity occupies centre stage and requires of the analyst a remarkable capacity for living in uncertainty. The likelihood is high that in the clinical process, particularly with some patients, both real need is expressed, and along with it, a curious species of camouflage, the blackwashing of need – neediness.

The relation between good need and bad need is inter-animating; each, at least sometimes requiring the other to make itself viable. When is a need not a need? When it's a need. If needs require camouflage then to all intents and purposes what you see is what you get; the actor seems identical to his part. There is, though, Ghent makes clear, 'genuine need', but something has happened in the early relationship that has, as it were, formed and fashioned these needs in a certain way. Ghent's language is theatrical:

The neediness by being easily confounded with genuine need, is well designed to keep the real need from being known by the analyst, let alone the patient. It is often expressive of true self, whereas neediness, garbed in protective coloration, is the impersonator.

This combination of military and theatrical vocabulary is instructive. We might have thought that there was an original pure thing called a need, or a true self, and this got disguised by neediness or a false self for reasons to do with early relationships. And this is certainly one clear implication of Ghent's (and Winnicott's) position. And yet an actor impersonating Hamlet, garbed as Hamlet, is only in a paradoxical sense impersonating him, because there is no original. The actor on the stage is Hamlet and not Hamlet; he is as much Hamlet as anybody is ever going to be, and he is not Hamlet at all. For some people, or for all people at some times, need will take the form of neediness, but there is no other form it could take. It exists, like an actor, only in the parts it plays. When we see Hamlet we don't ask ourselves is this really Hamlet, we ask ourselves how effective, how persuasive is this actor, this performance of Hamlet. This, Ghent implies, is what the analyst should be asking about the so-called needs of her patient. 'My reason for using the word "paradoxical" here', Ghent writes,

> is that two equally valid but contradictory statements apply; there is no need; what looks like need is a manipulative, at times vengeful demandingness, which is, in large measure, an expression of rage at lifelong deprivation of one form or another ... On the other hand there is need – genuine longings for human warmth, empathic responsiveness, trust, recognition, faith, playful creativity – all the ingredients we think of when we speak of love.

You will notice that sexuality is not mentioned by name in this list of genuine needs, though it may be entailed by all the things Ghent does mention. Perhaps it is worth suggesting that there is nothing more paradoxical, to use Ghent's term, than sexuality; nowhere in human experience where need and neediness are so successfully blurred and blended. And that is exactly why it should be celebrated. It is always the wrong question to ask about our sexual desire, is it true or false, is it need or neediness, is it good or bad. Like the actor who plays Hamlet, it is both because it is neither. Our sexuality may be the ultimate artefact of our being. So we might say that it has been the attempt among psychoanalysts to distinguish the good sexuality from the bad sexuality that has been so divisive; and that sexuality should be acknowledged to be a paradox rather than resolved as a contradiction. And this too would have consequences for the practice of psychoanalysis. And Ghent, I think, is on to them.

'It is difficult', he writes,

> to maintain the tension of appropriate response to these opposing expressions of need. One attempts to respond to what one feels is genuine need, especially when one senses the need emerging in forms that the patient is unaware of. I think of this type of response

as validation of real need, rather than as 'gratification', which I look upon as belonging more to the area of demand.

To validate is to acknowledge as significant; to gratify, in these terms, is to defuse or placate and so to perpetuate the failure of recognition. You might say psychoanalysis is the relationship in which validation and its consequences are explored, as opposed to so-called gratification and its consequences. One may not need to have very sophisticated or elaborate discussions about boundary disputes and the role of the analyst; one might just say, this is the place where we do this and not that. We may think and feel and say all sorts of things, but it is that form of recognition that Ghent calls validation – and that might also be called acknowledgement – that we have agreed to work at. When Ghent is doing what he calls 'separating meanings' that 'in practice ... often blend', he also, of course, implicitly invites us to blend any of his proposed oppositions. If, a bit too sternly, we want to separate out gratification from validation, we might also wonder what their blending might entail. If good need and bad need can be inextricable, so too perhaps can gratification and validation. Ghent allows us such thoughts, even when he doesn't explicitly promote them. 'This capacity for tolerating and living with paradox', he writes, 'is closely related to what I think of as acceptance. Resignation, by contrast, is the impersonator of acceptance.' This may be a comment addressed as much to the analyst's relationship with himself as practitioner, and with his colleagues, as it is a developmental aim for the patient. How much acceptance is going to be possible from a psychoanalytic point of view, when psychoanalysis itself depends upon the category of the unacceptable? Perhaps this is also a covert critique of the more dogmatic schools of analysis. Perhaps certain versions of Freudianism and Kleinianism are a schooling in resignation rather than acceptance.

It would not be merely provocative to say that Ghent's great paper *Masochism, Submission, Surrender*, is, among many other things, a paper as much about psychoanalytic training as about psychoanalytic treatment. About whether it is possible to conceive of a psychoanalytic training that is not, in however liberal a way, a Procrustean bed; and a psychoanalytic treatment that is not a cramping of the patient's personal style. There is a sense in which what is being fought over here is the nature of need and needing. Do the members of a psychoanalytic training institution or the practising analyst need to know what people need, or is that the problem masquerading as the solution? A lot of infant research is a quest for the grail of basic human need, suggesting as it does that needs can be discovered if only we can find the right research methods. It may, after all, be the case that what people have suffered as children is too definitive a decision about what they needed, negatively as deprivation, positively as impingement.

'The term interpersonal relations', Ghent writes in his credo,

in its deeper meaning refers to the non-fetishistic analysis of character, and only in a superficial sense to the colloquial 'what goes on between people'. Sullivan and Marx held in common the concept that consciously or unconsciously everything of value and importance in human life has meaning only in terms of man's relation to man.

Nothing about people has been more fetishised than the nature of their needs. A fetish, Ghent writes by way of clarification, 'obscures the relations between people ... in classical analysis such concepts as id, ego, superego likewise

"A ROSE IS A ROSE" DOES NOT GET YOU HALF OR TWO-THIRDS OF THE WAY TO "A ROSE IS A ROSE IS A ROSE". THERE IS ONLY ALL THE WAY THERE OR NOWHERE NEAR THERE.

obscure and mystify the underlying relation between people. They are fetishes. One might say that the id is the fetishistic formalisation of early experience.' Needs, one might say in certain descriptions, can be like the fetishes inside the fetish; <u>their mystification being in the way they seem to clarify so-called human nature.</u> In my reading of Ghent's paper, it is through what he calls surrender that a person can discover the personal nature of his own need (and that needing is an ongoing process and therefore not subject to finalised formulation); and that it is through submission that a person reinforces the fetishisation of his need.

There could be a whole conference on this paper, and in order to make my use of this object I have to be selective. But it is not incidental that as Ghent struggles to get at what he is getting at in this paper he has recourse to the notion of need. 'I have already hinted at the notion', he writes,

that these phenomena I am encompassing as surrender are not mere descriptions of a particular way of functioning, but are as well characterised by a quality of need, mostly operating out of awareness, yet seemingly with a relentlessness that is not easy to account for in traditional psychoanalytic terms. By 'need' I am not implying that there is something like an inborn instinct for the integration of self. My view is rather that in normal development the most primitive needs and functions of the infant, when adequately responded to and interacted with by the environing others, give rise to ever more sophisticated and complex conative structures, which later we recognise as having the valence or motivational quality of need.

Our fundamental need, Ghent says, is to be able to live in a way that enables our needs to come to light. It is notable that when Ghent gives, as he quite often does, his own list of basic needs – to be known, penetrated, affirmed, recognised, nurtured, etc. – they all describe facilitation not prescription or foreknowledge; these are not instrumental actions to known ends. A need for Ghent is an experiment rather than a fetish. He is keen to stress that by 'need' he does not, as he says, mean that there is 'something like an inborn instinct for the integration of the self'. After all, what could be more fetishistic than the whole notion of integration? It would be like knowing beforehand that all the parts could be fitted together (it would be possible to say: if there was such a thing as integration, there would be no such thing as psychoanalysis). One's need as an infant, Ghent suggests – and it is, perhaps, the only need he reifies – is to interact with an environment that allows for and encourages the discovery, as a continual process throughout life, of what one will learn to call in this culture one's needs. 'Surrender', Ghent writes, 'might be reflective of some force towards growth for which, interestingly, no satisfactory English word exists. Submission, on the other hand, either operates in the service of resistance or is at best adaptive as an expedient.' Submission, that is to say, is another word for the fetishising of need. It is the imposition, or self-imposition, of a fixed description of one's need. 'The main hypothesis of this paper', Ghent writes with his characteristic clarity,

is that it is this passionate longing to surrender that comes into play in at least some instances of masochism. Submission, losing oneself in the power of the other, becoming enslaved in one or other way to the master, is the ever available lookalike to surrender. It holds out the promise, seduces, excites, enslaves and, in the end, cheats the seeker turned victim of his cherished goal, offering in its place only the security of bondage and an ever amplified sense of futility. By substituting the appearance and trappings of surrender for the authentic experience, an agonising, though at times temporarily exciting masquerade of surrender occurs; a self-negating submissive experience in which the person is enthralled by the other.

The intensity of the masochism is a living testimonial of the urgency with which some buried part of the personality is screaming to be exhumed. This is not to be minimised as an expression of the longing to be healed, although so often we bear witness to its recurring miscarriage.

That is, I think, an astonishing piece of writing. We might differentiate psychoanalytic theories (or theorists) according to whether they require of us our submission, or our surrender. And of course Ghent counsels us, shrewdly, to distinguish things in order to better acknowledge that nothing lives in such stark states of distinction. We are likely to see submission and surrender together. I think Ghent's paper has a paradoxical effect that is integral to its subject matter. I can't help but surrender to this paper; I don't feel I am submitting to anything, because it is inspiring rather than informative; and yet there's something enthralling about it. But then it may also be part of the preconditions for surrender that one is moved to work out just what it might be that one is enthralled by; and this, one could say, is where psychoanalysis comes in. That we have a sense of being buried alive in our lives – 'some buried part of the personality is screaming to be exhumed' – that masochism might be a self-defeating performance of the wish to surrender; these are descriptions and propositions it would have been a great shame to have missed.

Everybody says nowadays in psychoanalysis that no one has access to ultimate truth. But only Ghent has said, as far as I know, that what he believes is that 'no one has a lien on ultimate truth'. A lien is a legal term meaning 'a right to retain possession of property until a debt due to the person detaining it is satisfied'. Ghent is full of surprises. He believes 'that no one has a lien on ultimate truth. Even as I portray the difference of viewpoints in this paradoxical way, I am aware that further complexities abound.' Ghent's paradoxical way, that actually wants further complexities to abound, is more than cause for celebration.

TRYING TO SEPARATE WHAT YOU ARE 'HEARING' FROM WHAT SOMEONE IS 'SAYING' COULD BE ONE WAY OF 'TALKING' TO YOURSELF.

Making It Old

Living in history but not living in the past.
Charles Wright, 'Chickamauga'

In E. M. Forster's novel *Howard's End* there is a scene in which, to initiate their courtship, the businessman Mr Wilcox takes Margaret Schlegel to Simpson's in the Strand for lunch. Margaret is not used to restaurants like this but she is involved in a kind of conversion experience to Mr Wilcox's belief in business, and so with the versions of the past that this belief in business recruits to sustain itself. '... while Mr Wilcox made some preliminary enquiries about cheese her eyes surveyed the restaurant', Forster writes, 'and admired its well-calculated tributes to the solidity of our past. Though no more Old English than the works of Kipling it had selected its reminiscences so adroitly that her criticism was lulled, and the guests whom it was nourishing for imperial purposes bore the outer semblance of Parson Adams or Tom Jones.' There is, as Forster makes clear, the past that people have arranged for us, and with purposes in mind, more or less imperial. It is, if it is done persuasively and well, a well-calculated tribute to the past, if not to the past's solidity. Indeed these days it is more likely to be a well-calculated tribute to the ways in which what we call the past has nothing that we can call solidity.

Whether it is in restaurants or galleries, or reading lists or history books, or television costume dramas, a past has been arranged for us – 'reminiscences adroitly selected' – in which an individual or a group or an institution agree to persuade us that this particular version and bit of the past should matter to us now. This provisionally consensual past will carry a range of conscious and unconscious projects with it. It may be literally trying to sell us something, but it will be trying to convince us of the value of something. It will have what Keats calls a 'palpable design' on us: it directs our attention and tries to fashion our sense of ourselves, and what these selves are supposed to want. But however seductive or persuasive or convincing this exhibition, this narrative, this costume drama is, its coercions are tempered by whatever else is going on inside ourselves at the time.

Keats went to medical lectures and found himself day-dreaming about poetry; Freud went to the opera to think about psychoanalysis; and we have all come here to talk and listen about the presence of the past. And yet something else, lots of various other things, are going on in what we call our minds. The question is, what are these other things, which are also coming from the past because there is nowhere else that they could come from? Psychoanalysis would call all these thoughts and feelings and apparent distractions and attractions, unconscious desire. And psychoanalysis would call unconscious desire itself a form of memory. Our preoccupations are the way our pasts go in search of a future. From a psychoanalytic point of view memory is of desire; we are formulating, we are picturing, in what we call our memories disguised descriptions of previous and longed-for satisfactions and terrors. In other words, when a person enters a gallery their own unofficial, largely unconscious past meets, meets up with, representations of a past that has been arranged for them. One is always bringing ones own past to the past.

145

Indeed there is, Freud seems to suggest, a desire for memory. We seem to want to, as it were, get bits of our past back, but in a very unscholarly way. There is the past we decide, more or less methodically, to find out about; we may research it, we may go to a gallery, we can read books. And this feels more like a choice. I may not know why I am interested in the French Revolution, and I may not need to know why, but I know how to go about finding out about it. We have some idea of what constitutes evidence of this more official, legitimate past that is a subject called history. But the unofficial past usually takes us by surprise; a song, a smell, a dream, a colour, a shape can take us back, unsuspecting. There is, in other words, the past we can research and pursue, and the past that springs on us. There is the past that can seem to be searching us out, while we go in search of other pasts. There is the idiosyncratic past and the more consensual past. So when we talk about the presence of the past we may need to remember – to include in our calculations – the unpredictable personal past that lurks in the pasts that are prepared for us by our curators and teachers and writers. An informative object is not necessarily an evocative object. When, in Forster's words, reminiscences are so adroitly selected that criticism is dulled, it is the past as propaganda that is being described. What Forster calls criticism here we could just call our relative freedom to have our own thoughts and feelings about what is on offer. The freedom to dream rather than merely imitate or repeat. From a psychoanalytic point of view the challenge for the curator or the historian is how to adroitly select reminiscences so that reminiscence is not dulled.

Trauma is when the past is too present; when, unbeknownst to oneself the past obliterates the present. It is the traumatised person – all of us, to some extent – who says that there is nothing new under the sun; that nothing ever changes. It is the art of art to make the past bearably present so that we can see the future through it. The problem, in other words, is not in making the past present, but in making the past into history.

Childhood Again

The typical intention has no morally interesting life
of its own.
Warren Quinn, *Morality and Action*

'You may or may not believe me,' Althusser writes in his autobiography, inviting a scepticism he wants to foreclose, 'but neither here nor elsewhere have I any intention of engaging in "self-analysis". I shall leave that to those clever people who like to indulge in "analytical theory" worthy of their private obsessions and fantasies. I am simply recording the various emotional experiences which marked me for life, both the earliest ones and those which occurred subsequently and were linked to them.' Althusser is clearly in at least two minds here. He won't be doing any 'self-analysis' using 'analytical theory' – at least he has no intention of doing that – but he will be recording the earliest emotional experiences that marked him for life. And he notably doesn't say that it will be those significant earlier and later experiences, but the later experiences which were linked to the earlier ones. It is, of course, that kind of link that the clever people who indulge in 'analytical theory' are most interested in. From a psychoanalytic point of view – with which Althusser was more than familiar through his work with Lacan, and the 'psychiatric experiences' that punctuated his life – the experiences of adulthood were only meaningful, were indeed only experiences, in so far as they

148

linked up with the formative episodes of childhood. Virtually everything Althusser wrote disqualifies the possibility that there could be any 'simple recording' of anything, least of all childhood.

Althusser's autobiography, *L'Avenir dure Longtemps* (*The Future Lasts a Long Time*), studded as it is with negations, is not, he writes, 'a diary, not my memoirs, not an autobiography ... My aim is not to confuse matters; on the contrary, I wish to highlight the crucial and marked similarity of those emotional experiences which occurred at different points in my life and made me what I am.' But what makes those emotional experiences seem similar to him? And why is he predisposed, albeit rather assertively, to believe that in matters of personal recollection, lucidity – simple recording, highlighting – is possible? If his title implies that memory is anticipation, and that anticipation is endless, his refusal of the available genres – autobiography, memoir, diary, psychoanalysis – implies that he is writing something unprecedented. 'Alas, I am no Rousseau,' he writes; but in its self-styled vindication of personal criminality, as the account he has not been able to give of the murder of his wife due to his being held 'not to be responsible in juridico-legal terms', and its reiterated claim to originality, Althusser's book clearly comes out from under Rousseau's overcoat.

But it is Althusser's conviction about the 'crucial and marked similarity' of early and later emotional experiences, his belief in the links between them, that makes his remarkable anti-autobiography a virtually conventional Freudian account of a life. Childhood as the period of formative experience (and experience described as essentially sexual and emotional); and the distinctive matters of adulthood seen retrospectively as having their disguised foreshadowings in childhood. A life as an idiosyncratic repertoire of repetitions; and the account of the life always already ironised by the Freudian knowingness of the narrator. The details of a life, of course, can never be predicted; nor can the content or the exact working of the repetitions (what Althusser calls the similarities). But what can be assumed is that there will be repetitions, and that these repetitions found their initial (and initiating) forms in childhood. Is it possible after psychoanalysis, or indeed after Rousseau, to think of anything in adulthood that doesn't seem to have its prototype in childhood (or even infancy if one is a Kleinian); or anything in childhood that cannot be described as a precursor (a formative link) of significant, or even trivial adult experience? It is as though the Freudian developmental schema, even in its most anti-developmental versions, can, at least retrospectively, integrate everything into its descriptions. By privileging the anomalous – that which cannot be assimilated, the unconscious as beyond our accommodations to it – it too quickly becomes, in Althusser's term, the similar. Our lives may be turbulent, but it is a patterned, if not actually a structured turbulence. From a certain point of view, that is to say, *L'Avenir dure Longtemps* is a book riddled with the (modern) ideology of childhood.

'An ideology', Althusser wrote in 'Marxism and Humanism' in 1965, 'is a system (with its own logic and rigour) of representations (images, myths, ideas or concepts, depending on the case) endowed with a historical existence and role within a given society.' As an ideology of childhood, psychoanalysis has a system of dream-work and repetition, primary processed thinking, and a systematised set of privileged representations: the dream, the joke and the symptom, the concepts of the pleasure principle, the reality principle, the repetition compulsion, the screen-memory. The privileging of childhood and repetition – newly systematised but not invented by Freud – encodes, brings in its wake, as it were, what might be called in Freudian terms a latent political content.

In simple terms, the Freudian child suffers, so to speak, from an intensity of desire and an excess of vulnerability; and it was not, as Aries was among the first to show, that this was news about childhood. The news was in the need, beginning in the eighteenth century, to make the child an object of systematic knowledge. But by making adults essentially children, it is as though in psychoanalytic theory the two terms have disappeared into each other: 'There is nowhere', Lacan writes, 'where man's relationship to himself has been less elucidated, nor where his recognition has needed to rise to a challenge more crucial than the one which resonates in classical thought through the statement of Pascal: "a child is not a man".' Freud was to say that the ways in which a child was not a man were both definitive of what it was to be a child, and what, in fact, the child suffered from in being a child. The child's strongest wish is to grow up – to become like the adults – and yet the Freudian adult is, to all intents and purposes, a child. A child is not a man, but a man is (or is like) a child. Childhood, that is to say, in Althusser's terms, has become a system of representations from which no one can escape; there could be nothing more natural than for us to think of ourselves as fundamentally, in origin, children. Childhood as at once our supreme referent, and our supreme fiction. It is, in John Searle's terms, a 'brute fact' that we have all been children; but our descriptions of children – of how, as it were, childhood works inside us, of what constitutes childhood for us – are 'institutional facts'. So it is, perhaps, worth wondering what it is that Freud wants us to agree upon about childhood; and what role – the consequences, the performances, the coercions – these agreements might play for us. The science of child development has tended to obscure – sometimes with unwitting intent – the ideology of childhood that has been integral to the history of psychoanalysis. What the child 'wants', and what we want from 'childhood', are inextricable.

'The child', Althusser writes in his posthumously published 'Letters to D.', 'irrupts as a biological being within the system of the symbolic order.' There is, as it were, nowhere else for the child to irrupt into. But what the child will acquire, in the terms of the symbolic order (and there are no other terms), is memory. And memory for Freud is memory of desire; indeed, soon memory is the form desiring takes. 'A child suckling at his mother's breast', Freud writes in a famous announcement, 'has become the prototype of every relation of love. The finding of an object is in fact a refinding of it.' Memory is never redemptive in Freud, it is merely constitutive, necessary for (psychic) survival. Desire, in a sense, devolves into recollection; and the question, implicit for Freud, and explicit for his more interesting followers, is about the status, indeed the plausibility of there being an original object (or experience); of what the apparent referent of memories might be (it is possible, for example, that all that is ever refound is the possibility of refinding). But what is not in question among psychoanalysts of otherwise diverse persuasions, is that childhood is a source, and that memory and therefore repetition – whether strived for, evaded or unwittingly consummated – is an integral and ineluctable process in a life. The individual's future is made through an ongoing project of returns. The experiences of childhood – if that is what they are – are at once our most privileged and elusive referents.

Memory becomes the hope, in however disguised a form, of the possibility of satisfaction, in its most various of forms. And yet the ideology of childhood, revolving as it does around the axis of pain and pleasure, has also been a way of making us wonder in what sense, from one's own point of view, one has ever been a child. It is usually self-evidently difficult for adults to 'believe' that they were once babies, which is in itself uncanny; but one's own childhood, in which one acquired and developed a capacity for representation, can seem more like a dream than a documentary, with its odd highlights, and its persistent fadings. It is as though there is childhood, but not for us; that much of our so-called childhood was the experience of our parents, of the adults who looked after us. They, as it were, told us about it in their own way, as it was going on, but it was like a commentary on a programme we ourselves couldn't see. And yet what we experience, and narrate, and what seems to confirm our having had childhood experiences, are memories and repetitions: those 'similarities' to which Althusser referred, that gradually transform, through symbolic transformation, the irruption of infancy into a pattern.

If it is repetition that formalises the continuity, however disguised, between childhood and adulthood – that makes childhood as inner experience a persuasive story – then the whole notion of unrepeatable experience becomes confounding, because, from a psychoanalytic point of view, something only becomes an experience through repetition (the nightmare recreates the trauma to make it into something that actually happened to a particular person; and in that sense the nightmare is an attempt to construct the kind

of person who would be able to have that kind of experience). We may know, or know about, the repeating childhood, but what then of the experiences of childhood that
have no echoes, that are neither foreshadowings nor pre-
parations? It is, in short, only the traumas of childhood –
only childhood as trauma – that psychoanalysis (and
psychoanalytic theory) can tell us about. What happens, to
put it pragmatically, to the experiences of childhood that are
not traumatic? This is not merely to reinstate the so-called
innocence of childhood – after all, what could be more
traumatic, more wholly daunting, than a happy childhood?
– but to acknowledge what might have happened to us as
children, but that was neither lost (and therefore needed to
be mourned), nor disturbing (and therefore needing to be
repressed). What we as adults might call the child's taken-
for-granted childhood would not so much be beyond
representation, but more simply not requiring of it (it
would use the representation it needed at the time, and
then relinquish it). A lot of our childhood, that is to say, may
be blank to recollection not merely because it is repressed,
but because it was, to all intents and purposes, blank at the
time. Children need only what we call internal worlds –
processes of symbolic transformation, ideologies – when
they are troubled by something. The relatively untroubled
periods of the child's lived life are of no interest; interest is
not required to make them into experiences. It is one of the
perils of so-called child analysis that it can traumatise the
child by foisting interest upon him; that is to say, making
meaning out of those things that don't need it. The making
of meaning is the sign of trauma; where one finds oneself
making it is the site of trauma.

'Forgetting impressions, scenes or experiences nearly
always reduces itself to shutting them off,' Freud writes in

'Remembering, Repeating and Working Through', but '"forgetting" becomes still further restricted when we assess at their true value the screen-memories which are so generally present ... Not only *some* but *all* of what is essential from childhood has been retained in these memories. It is simply a question of knowing how to extract it out of them by analysis.' But what *is* essential from childhood, and what do we think makes it so? It is extraordinary that someone might claim to be able to know, beforehand as it were, all of what is essential from childhood. It is not, of course, extraordinary, when what is essential is supposedly what is repressed. It is the idea of the unacceptable that makes the psychoanalytic ideology of childhood hang together. It is only the (in whatever sense) unacceptable – that which is the occasion for conflict – that the individual tries to rid himself of, and which returns disguised in the dream, or the symptom, or indeed the screen-memory. But what might be equally essential from childhood is that which has no need to return, which will be similar to nothing, but that informs our lives in ways that can only be acknowledged, but not described.

Perhaps something akin to what was once called negative theology might be useful here, so that one could say: everything that doesn't return is what is essential from childhood. We may then not need to go on – at least in quite the same way – plundering our lives, and our children, for childhood. Psychoanalysis, in other words, could teach us how to lose interest in our histories.

A Concentrated Rush

*The most successful career must show a waste of
strength that might have removed mountains, and the
most unsuccessful life is not that of the man who is
taken unprepared, but of him who has prepared and is
never taken.*

E. M. Forster, *Howards End*

Among the more telling revelations of Diana Trilling's
memoir, *The Beginning of the Journey*, are two journal entries
of her husband's that are about Hemingway. As private
journal entries they are perhaps appropriately confessional,
though Lionel Trilling, of course, was the least confessional
of critics; there is in his writing the always respectable
rhetoric of self-doubt, but there is no flaunting or fawning.
He is unerringly scrupulous about not demeaning himself.
Unlike the Dostoyevsky Trilling celebrated for his 'sacrifice
in himself of all the usual grounds of personal pride and
self-respect', he was never himself tempted, apparently, by
such a sacrifice. The journal entries, though, suggest otherwise. In a 1933 entry he describes a letter he has seen from
Hemingway to Clifton Fadiman. 'A crazy letter written
when he was drunk,' Trilling writes:

self-revealing, arrogant, scared, trivial, absurd: yet felt from
reading it how right such a man is compared to the 'good minds'
of my university life – how he will produce and mean something to
the world ... how his life which he could expose without dignity

156

and which is anarchic and 'childish' is a better life than anyone I
know could live, and right for his job. And how far-far-far I am
going from being a writer – and how less and less I have the
material and the mind and the will. A few – very few – more years
and the chance will be gone.

And then, in the same vein though written some thirty years
later, Trilling records his response to Hemingway's death
(in 1961). 'Except Lawrence's thirty two years ago,' he
writes, 'no writer's death has moved me as much – who
would suppose how much he haunted me? How much he
existed in my mind – as a reproach? He was the only writer
of our time I envied. I respected him in his most foolish
postures and in his worst work.' 'Who indeed would
suppose it?' Diana Trilling asks plaintively; 'Lionel's high
regard for Hemingway is more than a surprise, a shock.'
Trilling failed at his first and lasting ambition to be a fiction
writer. He had not fulfilled his 'literary vocation' of being a
novelist. 'Lionel', she writes, 'had not had the Bohemian
option – if that is what one wants to call it – of exposing his
life without dignity.'

In admitting, albeit to himself, his admiration for
Hemingway's anarchic and childish life which he was able
to expose without dignity; in respecting Hemingway's most
foolish postures, Trilling is himself acknowledging a furtive
wish to 'sacrifice in himself all the usual grounds of personal
pride and self-respect'. This, he intimates, is the sacrifice the
writer he envies is prepared to make, and the sacrifice that
the distinguished critic that he has become was unable or
unwilling to make. As though the critic, by definition as it
were, cannot be disreputable in his self-presentation. A critic
is someone who is the enemy of their own shame. Pride, the
fashioning of the self to then respect, can be a travesty;
the quest for identity a quest to betray one's desire.

That there is something one can refer to as 'the usual grounds of personal pride and self-respect' – that such things have grounds, and that they can be sacrificed – and that a failure to sacrifice such things has prevented Trilling from becoming the novelist he felt he had it in himself to be; these, I want to suggest, are among Trilling's abiding preoccupations – 'the continuing sense that wickedness', as he wrote in his journal in 1949, ' – or is it my notion of courage – is essential for creation'. And creation here means both the self-creation of everyday life, and the writing that can be integral to that more lived life.

'The continuing sense that wickedness – or is it my notion of courage – is essential for creation'; the inauthenticity of virtue, the confinements of pride and self-respect, the sense that there is less life in being good; that being good is good but being bad is better. These of course are not new ideas or characteristically modern forms of moral suspicion. Nor, of course, are they peculiarly Jewish concerns. And Trilling, even in his journal, exposes with dignity his buried desire to expose his life without dignity. And yet the idea that wickedness, at least for some people, might be another word for courage; or indeed that self-respect and personal pride could be forms of cowardice such that one might fear, above all, sacrificing them; these were Trilling's private and more obliquely public confessions. 'Mr Trilling does not confess failure', R. P. Blackmur remarked in his review of *The Liberal Imagination*; 'it is one of the freakish qualities of his mind that he does not make any confessions at all.' And then Blackmur goes on to quote something by Niebuhr that he tells us Trilling 'quotes approvingly': 'Radical Evil' is 'man's inclination to corrupt the imperatives of morality so that they may become a screen for the expression of self-love'. Morality as a screen for self-love; and that version of self-love – call it pride or self-respect – as the saboteur of Hemingway's 'better life' and better writing. If Hemingway's 'crazy letter' is 'self-revealing, arrogant, scared, trivial, absurd ... anarchic ... "childish"' – as good a description as any of many of the heroes of Bellow and Roth – and these are qualities for the more private Trilling, then we cannot help noticing that these are not the qualities we associate with the subjects of Trilling's first two books, Matthew Arnold and E. M. Forster. Trilling, that is to say, wrote his first books about writers who were, in a sense, quite at odds with his more private preferences. And given Trilling's own ambition to be above all a novelist, Forster, in the light of these considerations, might seem in particular to have been a strange first choice.

And yet we are told both by Trilling himself – who suffered throughout his life from writing blocks – and by his wife in her memoir, that writing about Forster released something in him. After the prolonged and partly dutiful drudgery of writing the Arnold, which began life as a Ph.D. thesis, Lionel, his wife writes, 'wrote his E. M. Forster with unaccustomed speed; it was finished in six weeks.' And Forster, as Diana Trilling is keen to tell us in her setting-the-record-straight book, wasn't even his 'favourite novelist ... the fact that Lionel wrote a book about Forster does not mean that he held him in this high esteem ... Forster never had the place in Lionel's affections of such novelists as Dickens, Dostoevsky, Tolstoy or Henry James or Jane Austen; at his most appreciative Lionel did not attribute to him the stature of these earlier writers. When he completed his study he did not return to him as a subject, nor do I recall his reading him for recreation.' In the Preface to his second edition of the Forster book, written in 1964, Trilling agrees and disagrees with his wife's account. 'Most

of the book was written, as I well remember, in a con-
centrated rush, and although much of the enthusiasm and
pleasure is to be attributed to my liking of the subject, I have
no doubt that I was benefited by the special energies that
attend a polemical purpose.' It was written fast, partly
because of the subject, and partly because Trilling was using
Forster for a polemical purpose. So I want to ask not exactly
why Forster, but akin to this, what was the pleasure Trilling
got from Forster, what about him could he enjoy, and where
was he drawn to take issue? How did Forster help him to
find what he could afford to believe? In what Jonathan
Freedman has called 'the assimilation-by-culture trail' of
modern American-Jewish novelists and critics, what made
Trilling choose this bit of the available modern literary
culture called E. M. Forster? Forster, that is, not being
Hemingway, nor an American, nor a Jew.

The idea that the things about yourself that you most
value – 'the grounds of personal pride and self-respect' – are
felt to be the problem of your life; indeed, need to be
sacrificed in order to have the better life of which you are
capable, is itself, paradoxical. If Trilling can see the virtue in
Hemingway's vices, it is because he can sense a kind of
duplicity in himself. As though, wittingly or unwittingly, he
is involved in a determined misrecognition of himself. He
stages it in terms of himself and the 'good minds' of his
university life as opposed to Hemingway, who could
expose his life without dignity, and himself as potential
novelist. Dignity is a form of self-possession; he and the
fellow good minds of his university life are too self-
possessed to be otherwise possessed.

'Tacitus', Trilling wrote in *The Liberal Imagination*, 'never
becomes the victim of what he writes about – he had too
much power of mind for that.' That, Trilling implies, is what

the mind is for; to prevent one from being a victim. And the mind, as we know, was the organ, was the term, that Trilling promoted in his criticism. I want to suggest that the avoidance of victimhood – and this would be one crude description of Trilling's whole critical project – precludes the experience of surrender. That vigilance of mind, the fear of submission – and this may have something to do with Jewish critics and modern culture – incarcerates the self. If not being a victim – in one's own eyes and in the eyes of others – becomes a paramount consideration, dignity must be privileged; the childish and the anarchic – in Trilling's post-romantic, Freudian allegory of the self – must be kept at bay. This, I think, is what Trilling was telling himself in his secret admiration for what he calls Hemingway's 'foolish postures' that both haunted him and reproached him about his buried life; he was telling himself, in no uncertain terms, what an aversion to submission pre-empts in the self. What the fear of surrendering oneself might exclude one from. And submission might cover here a range of experience; from childhood, from the ideological communism and Stalinism that Trilling cut his intellectual teeth on in the thirties, to what he called in an early essay the myth of the Jew.

'When the Jew, at the Emancipation, entered into the life of the Western World,' Trilling writes, 'he found the myths awaiting him. Sometimes he fought them, sometimes he accepted them to his own advantage, often he went off and contemplated them in great confusion of mind. When he came to write of himself he was not able to free himself from them. Being a Jew for Trilling meant not submitting to the myths of being a Jew. And this meant not fighting the myths, which would be to acknowledge that one was already victimised by them. And certainly not accepting them to his own advantage, which is to consent to them. Nor of course was Trilling keen to be seen in a state of great confusion of mind; mind, after all, was ideally for Trilling the solvent, the clarifier of its own confusions ('Mind does not move towards its ideal purposes over a royal straight road,' he writes in *Mind and the Modern World*, 'but finds its way through the thicket of its own confusions and contradictions'). It meant for Trilling what I can only call aestheticising defiance; making of defiance something so unbrash, something so ungauche, something at once stylish but apparently unself-regarding, that one could call it the liberal imagination, or, slightly more luridly, the opposing self. And this is where the very English liberal Forster comes in, who makes his first odd entrance in Trilling's book on Arnold. The Forster who, by his own admission, Trilling never recognised as gay.

Trilling is discussing, as usual, what he calls 'the human mind' – 'the human mind is far more complex than Arnold allows' – and how the great European literature of the past (*Faust*, *In Memoriam*, *The Waste Land*, Proust) has been 'based on the dialogue of the mind with itself', and that this has been 'illuminating and health giving'. And yet, Trilling goes on, moral hygiene and enlightenment may not be the be-all and end-all. 'We read to live,' he writes bracingly.

but we do not live only by the literature of resolution. The many ways in which literature can help us to live and the many ways it can clarify us are brilliantly suggested by E. M. Forster, who tells how, during the madness of the War, he found sanity in – of all books – Huysman's *A Rebours*!

'Oh the relief of a world which lived for its sensations and ignored the will ... Was it decadent? Yes, and thank God. Yes; here again was a human being who had time to feel and experience with his feelings, to taste and smell and arrange books and fabricate flowers, and be selfish and himself. The waves of edifying bilge rolled off me, the newspapers ebbed ...'

Huysman is not Hemingway; but what Forster is promoting for Trilling is another alternative to high-mindedness, the 'edifying bilge rolled off me'. Trilling, like Arnold, was not a great sponsor of decadence. But the sensuousness described – books as smellable objects – and the human being who had time to be 'selfish and himself' are not worlds apart from Trilling's drunken Hemingway and his foolish postures, 'self-revealing, arrogant, scared, trivial, absurd'. Forster is saying that during the war he needed relief from a certain kind of seriousness, a refuge from commitment and the more impressive personal ideals. It would be madness to take the war so seriously that one forgot the world of rather more pleasurable sensations.

This, one could say, represents the counter-aspiration – that presents itself as a kind of counter-life – in Trilling's writing. Forster is Trilling's opportunity, among other things, to find a respectable, legitimate decadence for himself. And the quest for a legitimate decadence, for a dignity of exposure, may be the necessary counter-life of the Jewish or any immigrant writer in modern culture.

There is, for Trilling, something relaxed and relaxing about Forster. 'The very relaxation of his style,' Trilling writes, 'its colloquial unpretentiousness, is a mark of his acceptance of the human fact as we know it now.' He admires Forster's 'belief in the relaxed will ... [and] deep suspiciousness of the rigid exercise of the intellect'. And as a critic he suggests Forster – 'a critic', he writes, 'with no drive to consistency, no desire to find an architectonic for his impressions' – as a contrast, a counter-weight, to Eliot. 'In Eliot,' he writes, the desire to make laws and the conscious effort for dignity have their unquestionable effect upon us. We respond to the effort; the form of dialectic gives us pleasure; we are connected with large issues. Literature thus acquires a magnificent importance, life seems more interesting. In such a critic we have met either an ally with whom we attack some enemy of the human spirit or an opponent who gives us the satisfaction of conflict. Forster, on the contrary, asks us to relax. He can tell us, and very movingly, of the importance of literature, but he never intends to make any single literary work important. And the manner of his presentation of ideas is personal in a way that mocks the erection of laws.

It is not too far-fetched to see the young Trilling using Eliot and Forster to stage a personal conflict of his own; Eliot's 'conscious effort for dignity', the serious grandeur of his critical project, set against Forster's invitation to relax, his personal presentation of ideas that, in Trilling's strange and cute phrase, 'mocks the erection of laws'; what Trilling calls in his book Forster's 'refusal of greatness'. In Trilling's description Eliot sounds the more impressive, Forster the more genial (if not entirely congenial to Trilling). It is the 'conscious effort for dignity' – that Trilling links with what he calls the mind, or the 'intellectual tradition'; and that is linked in turn with the inability to refuse greatness – that Trilling cannot quite resist. There is the lure of gravity, of strenuous moral commitments, and the temptations of an ordinary decadence. In the closing pages of his book Trilling joins Forster and Arnold as his secret sharers; as accomplices that, like Hemingway, he would have to betray. 'Perhaps no one in our time has expressed so simply as Forster', Trilling writes with apparently innocent complicity,

the weariness with the intellectual tradition of Europe which has been in some corner of the European psyche since early in the 19th century. The young Matthew Arnold felt, a hundred years ago, much of what Forster feels today. It was the perception of the dangers of a rigid intellectualism, a fierce conscience, the ever-lasting research of the mind into itself that made the young Arnold keep his distance from his Oxford friends and be aggressively gay, arrogant, frivolous, dandified, at the very time he was writing some of his best and saddest verse. He feared their nagging, rigorous intellects; he wanted the life of acceptant calm – he never said the life of simple instinct, but perhaps it was that too – into which the discriminating judgement did not always enter.

There is an obvious echo here of the journal entry about the Hemingway letter. Once again the 'good minds' of a university life are contrasted with, in Arnold's case, the 'aggressively gay, arrogant, frivolous, dandified' alternative. Whether or not Trilling identified with Arnold's thwarted creative life – and despite the fact that he would go on to write a novel – the passage sounds like another elegy for Trilling the novelist; a doomed resignation if not an acceptance of his fate as a critic. 'I am always surprised', he would write in 1971, 'when I hear myself referred to as a critic. After some thirty years of having been called by that name, the role and the function it designates seem odd to me ... The plan that did please my thought was certainly literary, but what it envisaged was the career of a novelist.'

What Trilling called his 'abiding intention' to be a novelist, the literary ambition not to be a critic, is somehow linked in his writing with a refused decadence, an absorption in the 'conscious effort for dignity'. And yet Trilling wants to celebrate Forster as above all a comic novelist: 'The comic manner', he writes, 'will not tolerate absolutes.' It is what he calls, in a telling phrase, Forster's 'serious whim' that he wants us to note. And he recruits Stendhal to say something odd about Forster as a comic and 'playful' novelist. 'Stendhal believed', Trilling writes, that gaiety was one of the marks of a healthy intelligence, and we are mistakenly sure that Stendhal was wrong. We suppose that there is necessarily an intellectual 'depth' in the deep tones of the organ; it is possibly the sign of a deprivation – our suspicion of gaiety in art perhaps signifies an inadequate seriousness in ourselves.

We are inadequately serious if we are suspicious of gaiety; but seriousness is clearly the thing. Lionel, Diana writes in her memoir, 'was not to be described as a happy person. Indeed, he thought poorly of happiness and of people who claimed to be happy or desired happiness above other gratifications in life ... Seriousness was the desirable condition of man, especially literary man.' Forster's comic manner that 'will not tolerate absolutes', that believes in good and evil and not their antagonism, is what recommends Forster to the young Trilling; the 'serious whim', the seriousness of Forster's moral complexity and playfulness. But it is the stressed seriousness that sustains Trilling's enthusiasm for Forster. What kind of work this keyword is doing here and now in Trilling's writing is of some significance. Because for Trilling, Forster represents an alternative version of seriousness to the liberalism that Trilling is already oppressed by. He can't bring himself to be Hemingway or the young dandified Arnold; but he can almost locate himself, like Forster the novelist, as a liberal against liberalism; 'indifference to the commonplaces of liberal thought makes the very texture of Forster's novels', Trilling writes in a sentence prophetic of his own writing.

And yet there is also in Trilling's account of Forster's liberalism a kind of negative prophecy – an implicit intimation of what Trilling would rarely let himself do in his own writing. 'We of the liberal connection', he writes with a certain disdain, have always liked to play the old intellectual game of antagonistic principles. It is an attractive game because it gives the sensation of thinking, and its first rule is that if one of two opposed principles is wrong, the other is necessarily right. Forster will not play this game; or rather, he plays it only to mock it.

It is not on the whole Trilling's way to mock; or rather he will ironise, as he does here, but he will resist ridicule. He will, in the liberal way that he is so ambivalent about, reason and persuade. Forster's seriousness, for Trilling, is in his mockery of the reasonableness of liberalism. Liberalism is for Forster, by its very nature, a subject for comedy.

Jonathan Freedman, in *The Temple of Culture*, describes Trilling as 'performing the equanimity that Jews, stereotyped as being passionate and overemotional, were accused of lacking'. The enemy of equanimity is humiliation; and irony is its guardian. If we remember Trilling's almost awestruck description of Dostoyevsky's 'sacrifice in himself of all the usual grounds of personal pride and self-respect'; or Hemingway's foolish postures, exposing his life without dignity; or the young Arnold, 'aggressively gay, arrogant, frivolous, dandyfied'; these are all celebrations of people leaving themselves open to ridicule. It is the imaginative cost of not leaving oneself open to ridicule that haunted Trilling; and that is perhaps integral to the fate of the Jewish writer in modern culture. What breaks out in the fictional heroes – though not heroines – of Bellow and Roth and Mailer are the more brazen performances of the self that Trilling could only resist.

One can, of course, unwittingly lay oneself open to ridicule; and much satire and parody is the exposure of apparent or unapparent naivety. But what Trilling was tempted by, I think – and which he connected with his life-long literary vocation as a failed novelist – was the more witting, the intended, perhaps even the forced exposure of his life without dignity, which Diana Trilling refers to, with veiled contempt, as the 'Bohemian option' that her husband did not have. The option he and others did have, however, was psychoanalysis, in which one is invited, as a therapeutic measure, to do precisely that; to abrogate one's 'conscious effort for dignity' in the service of something putatively better. But a psychoanalysis, like a journal, is a relatively private affair. It is a refuge for the exposure of one's life without dignity. It is neither public, nor published. One's 'childishness' is secluded. Trilling's celebration of Freud, that is to say, may be the cover-story for his failure as a novelist; whatever that makes psychoanalysis a cover-story for.

CHARACTERS

Svengali

First of all we have to imagine a world in which people suffer and have no hope that anything or anyone can make a difference. Then we have to imagine what it would be like to live in a world of people who have no wish to help each other or to feel better. If we don't do this, the history of medicine, and of its country cousin psychiatry, not to mention the history of religion, will hardly seem different from a history of quacks and con-artists ingeniously exploiting the hopelessly vulnerable. The question has always been: what, if anything, can be done? Only when we acknowledge the very real drawbacks of living in a world in which everyone's unhappiness renders everyone clueless, can we review our contemporary options and their histories with some sense of relief. We may have very real doubts now about, say, aromatherapy, or ECT, or cognitive psychology – or even about people having personal trainers – but we quite literally have to do something when we begin to feel in some way troubled. It is fortunate that pain has made us so inventive.

As unhappiness shows no sign of disappearing – and its staying power makes us look more like fashion victims than truth-seekers in our quest for therapies – we would do better to think of our solutions as inevitably provisional and uncertain, instead of sneering at them. We should be more cheerful followers of fashion, even if one of our best ways of following fasion is to resist it. Our misgivings about the

Review of Daniel Pick, *Svengali's Web: The Alien Enchanter in Modern Culture* (Yale University Press, 2000), from the *London Review of Books* available treatments for our contemporary miseries too easily turns into a cover-story for an intolerance of, or impatience with, suffering itself. Scepticism about treatments becomes suspicion about patients (if the treatment is fraudulent, and it works, then the condition it was nominally treating must be fraudulent too: so everyone's a fool). The contesting of cures, if it does nothing else, keeps the idea of cure alive; but it tends to make people in the so-called helping professions excessively judgmental of each other (i.e., rivalrous). On the other hand, the prestige involved in helping people has always been integral to the treatment, and it has been to the consumers and purveyors of charisma that historians and psychologists have increasingly turned their attention. As a psychoanalyst and a historian, Daniel Pick is unusually well-qualified to have written this often intriguing book.

The intricate complicity between symptoms and cures – and between what people are considered to be suffering from and what they claim to be suffering from – has made the history of medicine, in its broadest sense, of so much recent interest. Part of the fascination (so to speak) of mesmerism and hypnosis – and of the history that is so well told in *Svengali's Web* – is that, as potential cures for a wide range of miseries, they were so quickly seen to be at once remarkable breakthroughs, and disreputable, if not criminal activities. It was not clear whether (like the psychoanalysis that was born of this tradition) they were solutions, or problems in themselves, or both. Indeed for some people, the fact that these forms of treatment helped the patient was itself the patient's most serious and revealing symptom; and what it revealed was the patient's pathological naivety. People were not being cured through hypnosis, the critics said, they were suffering from being hypnotisable: what they really needed to be cured of was their susceptibility to certain cures. These new treatments, in other words, had ironically disclosed what some feared might be the most terrible, perhaps the most constitutively human problem of all: that people could have considerable influence over each other. That bodies affected each other in daunting and undreamt of ways; that eyes and voices and hands – among other body-parts – were essentially rhetorical organs. That modern people wanted above all to *feel* alive, not to think that they were alive, or have to prove it.

Both as a theatrical spectacle and as a medical treatment, hypnotism made it clear that bodies were persuasive, and that the appetite for persuasion and for being persuaded was exorbitant. It may seem odd, in retrospect, that this should have seemed so shocking. Christianity, after all, was an extravagant acknowledgement of the power of the body; and sexuality, through its various historical formations and deformations, has always been spoken of as a fascination (sex, too, has a reputation for being the problem and the solution). But what the hypnotist exposed, perhaps most devastatingly in such a progressive age as the nineteenth century, was just how lowbrow people really were. It wasn't truth or goodness they were after: they wanted to be moved. And it wasn't exactly the other person's logic, or their argument, or the information they provided or even their education that was convincing, so much as the look in their eye or their smile. As many commentators – then as now – were quick to point out, this makes politics more volatile than some want it to be, and science much less influential than some think it should be.

The hypnotist and his subject were like a tableau, or a ✳ model, of something fundamental and disturbing about human nature. If we are sensual but not that sensible – if we only feel and are barely rational – then hypnotism is not much more than another word for human relations. The question was no longer, could hypnotism be disproved (and therefore discredited), but what was the alternative? What did people do together that wasn't hypnotism, or horribly akin to it? If politics, religion and sexual relations couldn't easily exempt themselves from such a dismaying comparison, why should medicine be able to? Hypnotism was like a terrible cartoon – a secular revelation – of the power people could have over each other, of the enthralled longing to be free from choice. Seeing the amazing things bodies could do to each other – witnessing just how manipulable people's limbs and memories were – made hypnotism as a phenomenon endlessly fascinating, if not actually hypnotic. Since the turn of the last century it has been assumed, or hoped, that a combination of science and history might break its spell. In its sober speculation, and its wealth of often fascinating research, *Svengali's Web* is in this honourable but somehow forlorn tradition of lucid and intelligible enquiry into unfathomable craziness.

It is the contention of Pick's book that Du Maurier's once extremely famous novel, *Trilby*, with its evil, hypnotising Jew, Svengali, was a sensation waiting to happen; and that we have to go back to the beginnings of mesmerism in the eighteenth century, and forward to the advent of psychoanalysis at the turn of the last century, to understand why. The ground, as Pick shows in impressive detail, had been cleared – or rather, given the many theatrical adaptations of *Trilby*, the stage had been set – for this particular bestseller. Wittingly or unwittingly, Du Maurier had tuned into the spirit of the age, and turned up the volume. *Trilby*, as Pick says, 'is generally thought to have been the bestselling novel of the last century'; and this alone makes it, for better and for worse, what used to be called a 'symptomatic text': a way into the multiple overlapping histories of race and gender and science and pseudo-science in the nineteenth century. *Svengali's Web*, in other words, is topical by academic standards; and is, in its turn, something of a symptomatic text itself.

What Pick uses cultural history to do is integral to his subject. And one of the things he uses it for is to promote a not unfamiliar progress myth – it was more or less Freud's own myth and so became, more or less, the official line – in which the follies of mesmerism and hypnosis are displaced by the stronger rationality of psychoanalysis. When Freud abrogates hypnosis as a therapeutic technique, psycho-analysis is born, and the nineteenth century begins to see sense where previously there had only been the hocus-pocus of suggestion. In Freud's writing, Pick intimates, meaning is finally derived from all the bewildering psycho-pathology of everyday life. 'Freud', he writes, 'was soon to conceptualise much of the psychic terrain and unspeakable desires to which other writers of the period seemed to be vaguely alluding ... Such a vocabulary remained out of reach for Du Maurier.' But because Pick insists that *Trilby* is a very poor novel, and that psychoanalysis was (and is) a very great clarification; because he is curiously snobbish about 'popular culture', and needlessly defensive of psy-choanalysis, nuances are lost in what is otherwise an engaging book.

'Psychoanalysis', Pick writes, 'is painted by its critics as a historical monolith, entirely unreconstructed since its inception, as though Freud *was* Svengali and the entire movement his helpless Trilby.' But this is to take a mono-lithic view of the critics. Proving that Freud was not Svengali is less promising than wondering why (and whether) this needs to be disproved. And the best critics of psychoanalysis are rather more interesting than Pick suggests, pointing out, as some of them do, that there are many ways of hypnotising people – saying very little and sitting out of sight is one – and that Freud's so-called movement has been rather more of a cult than his followers have been prepared to admit. The interesting question is what is it about psychoanlysis that stops it being a form of hypnosis? Pick uses *Trilby* to answer this question, or at least to go some way towards doing so, making the whole issue into a kind of contest between the vulgar and the more refined, between the entertainers and the better educated. 'All of Du Maurier's novels,' Pick writes, 'to say nothing of the spoofs and speculations which followed, epitomised a maudlin and melodramatic style of the day that many grander critics and philosophers despised. Yet in the figure of the exploitative, beguiling conductor and his touching victim, Du Maurier had hit on a curiously resonant symbol.' *Svengali's Web* is about how such a thing could have happened.

Trilby, first published in 1894, is the story of Trilby O'Ferrall, whom we first meet as an artist's model, and friend of three bohemian British artists living and working in Paris. She has her own terrible history as the orphaned daughter of alcoholic parents. In flight from horrible memories she is – it soon becomes obvious – in desperate need of something; she has, the narrator tells us, 'a singularly impressionable nature, as was shown by her quick and ready susceptibility to Svengali's hypnotic influence'. Svengali, the archetypal alien enchanter of Pick's title, eases her pain, as well as facilitating a seemingly astonishing talent. In Henry James's well chosen words, Trilby is 'mesmerised and made to sing by a little foreign Jew who has mesmeric power, infinite feeling, and no organ (save as an accompanist) of his own'. It is a story about exploitation, possession and artistry, and very self-consciously of its time. It is a strange and artful book; and Du Maurier seems to me more archly attentive to what he is up to than Pick gives him credit for. When, for example, the narrator describes the talk of these young bohemian artists as not 'redolent of the very highest culture (which, by the way, can mar as well as make)', Du Maurier is clearly drawing attention to the relationship between marring and making, and how this might figure in the art of his own book. Perhaps unsurprisingly, given that Du Maurier was a friend of James's and discussed the plot of *Trilby* with him, the novel is riddled with questions about high and low art. Pick's 'aim', he says, 'has been to set out the available intellectual, cultural and political ingredients' from which Du Maurier 'concocted so idiosyncratic and influential a recipe'. And although he achieves this, it is almost at the cost of any kind of close reading of the novel itself. In fact, one of the curious things about *Svengali's Web* is that Pick seems determined to persuade us that *Trilby* is not worth reading – except, that is, for the cultural history that a sufficiently informed reader can unpack from it.

What makes *Trilby* such a bad book in Pick's eyes is its 'mawkishness as well as the insistent "anti-high culture tone"' – quite apart from the fact that 'Du Maurier was no Proust'. For 'anti-high culture tone', I think we should read 'questions about high culture, and 'questions about what it might be to be anti-high culture'; if *Trilby* is alert to anything it is alert to what is done in the name of art and culture. And if we are still in any doubt about the novel's real worth, Pick assures us that 'Du Maurier certainly has some eminent detractors. The highly distinguished literary critic, Professor Frank Kermode, for example, finds precious little to admire in Du Maurier's writing.' Perhaps Pick wants to protect us (and himself) from the blandishments of the book. One can't be fastidious enough with this novel. 'If the laboured pathos of the story now causes us to flinch,' Pick writes – again underestimating Du Maurier's shrewd sense of genre – 'it should be remembered that many of Du Maurier's contemporaries were as deeply absorbed and affected by the novel's themes as they were keen to buy *Trilby* accessories.' Using so-called popular culture as a pretext for highbrow commentary has its dangers, of course, the most obvious of which being that it makes the people who enjoy popular culture seem somehow deficient. By dividing the world into the informed and the uninformed – and especially when doing so with historical hindsight – cultural historians easily make themselves sound merely ahead of the game. Even though, as Pick himself points out, Svengali is finally exposed as a fraud, 'the enigma remained: how was one to explain Svengali and company's massive cultural appeal?' Does that mean that fraudulence only exists in so far as it can be exposed? 'The tale had something extraordinary about it,' Pick continues, 'a passion had been unleashed in excess of any evident logic, and for reasons that had little to do with literary merit.' The idea of literary merit, like the idea of fraudulence, depends on surenesses of judgement that the author of *Trilby*, among others – and Freud was among those others – knew to be under pressure. At the height of his success with Trilby, Svengali showed just how precarious personal judgement is. Hypnotism makes a mockery of good taste. Which is another thing it might share with psychoanalysis. Psychoanalysis, of course, as a profession allows people with often rather high-brow tastes to flirt with disreputable things.

How can so many people – even 'intelligent' people –

think bad things are good? the old-fashioned intellectual cries. Or even worse, not care whether they are good or bad, but just want them? That people want things that apparently do them harm – that they can desire the unimproving thing – might make us wonder less about human depravity and rather more about the points that pleasure makes. Pick seems keener to fight a rearguard action for literary merit than to want to rethink it. And this is strange because *Svengali's Web* is everywhere interested in, and interesting about, the threats to social cohesion posed by alien enchanters of various kinds, and about the implications of this for ideas about the making of a political or aesthetic consensus. If, as he says, 'the alien hypnotist also became a kind of conduit for a much wider contemporary unease concerning the nature of irrational social influences and psychological transmissions,' then any kind of social rule, or standard, any attempt to set limits or draw boundaries, is under threat. And there could be no more vivid evidence of these irrational influences and transmissions than cultural fads and crazes and fashions, like *Trilby* itself. Then as now, the anguish aroused by hypnotism was that it revealed all too starkly the ways in which people could be enthused and impressed and persuaded – and even deranged and virtually (or literally) kidnapped – in spite of themselves. Our conscious choices, it suggested, may be as nothing compared with our unconscious (unknown beforehand) powers of discrimination. The problem for the newly emerging nineteenth-century democrat was that to disdain popularity was to disdain people. <u>If culture wasn't popular, why should it be called culture?</u> And yet the art of capturing the public imagination, as Pick makes abundantly clear, could seem like a very dark art indeed.

It is not, of course, obvious why it would have been better

– or indeed what the consequences might have been – if the passions unleashed by *Trilby* had been due to its literary merit rather than its supposed demerit. When Pick writes that 'those tempted to become involved in seances and to succumb to trances were in very good company indeed. Numerous writers, artists and scientists had plunged in at the deep end, not only as patients but as would-be practitioners,' it is not evident who is being reassured about what. Did the presence of these writers and artists and scientists in some way legitimate these practices, or just show that these distinguished people were as seducible, as impressionable, as everyone else? After all, the thing about hypnotism and its paranormal spin-offs – indeed part of their fascination – was that they played havoc with apparently established hierarchies of class, gender and profession. Everyone, it seemed, was suggestible. Man, as he was then called, was the animal who wanted to seduce and be seduced.

Science – in the form of psychology, anthropology, biology – was mobilised, as Pick shows, by mesmerism and hypnosis to explain what we now call seduction. But with the background fear – that has turned out to be largely justified – that explaining seduction might not make a difference to its prevalence or its power; that it may in fact just be another form that seduction can take (people could be usefully said to have been hypnotised by science, and so none the wiser). It's just possible that hypnotism is the best description we have so far come up with for what goes on between people, whether we are talking about parents and children, doctors and patients, or nations and their leaders. This, Pick implies, is what made *Trilby* take: not that Svengali was a fraud (the existence – and exposure – of fraudulence is itself taken to be proof that somewhere there is a genuine, trustworthy, reliable person), but that such essential distinctions may no longer hold, or that we are no longer interested in making them. The alien enchanter may be longed for as much as he is feared. And it is in writing about the Jew as alien enchanter – with Svengali as the modern prototype – that Pick's book is at its best.

There were – and Pick quotes them well – many Victorian writers, of varying professions, who were keen to argue that 'the "virtues and vices" of ... the Jews included special powers of psychic manipulation'; and that they were 'especially prone to the sort of volatile emotional and hypnotic states in which deadly impulses are acted upon'. A Jew like Svengali, 'well-featured but sinister', as Du Maurier describes him, a brilliant musician and a versatile linguist, at once redeeming and ruining a vulnerable gentile girl, couldn't avoid being a dramatic contribution to a topical debate. In both the popular press and the specialist medical journals, what Pick calls 'the figurative bond between mesmerism and the Jews' became increasingly prominent throughout the nineteenth century. In such widely read magazines as *Punch*, 'later Victorian Jews were often represented as "Svengalian" – ingratiating, seductive, dangerously alluring ... not only as repulsive, but also as psychologically penetrating.' What Pick demonstrates above all is the astonishing confusion that Jews evoked in the English. 'In the wider culture,' he writes, 'they were often said to confound the gentile, to produce an intolerable bafflement.' The bafflement, it seems, was largely about themselves. 'The repeated perception of the Jews as effective healers but also as potentially lethal magicians' vied with what Pick calls 'the fear of the Jew's capacity to transform weakness into strength'. Whether they were regarded as 'highly equivocal figures, the bearers of poisons and remedies', or whether the English couldn't tolerate their own deep-seated (if not actually enthroned) ambivalence, all Pick's documentation suggests that the Jews in England in the nineteenth century created a conflict in their hosts but not, fortunately, the dire intolerance, found later and elsewhere. If Disraeli and Fagin and Svengali shared a certain caricature in England, as Pick suggests, it was chaotically uncertain of its own values.

It has been the project of most anti-semites, and some of their critics, to make the Jews into a special case: chosen again either as uniquely fascinating or exceptionally depraved; unusually talented or uniquely scurrilous. What Pick manages to do in *Svengali's Web* is to place a great deal of primary source material on mostly British nineteenth-century anti-semitism alongside a lucid overview of the more convincing theoretical attempts to make sense of what is, by any standards, bizarre and equivocal material. 'Loaded', in Pick's words, 'with particularly paradoxical meanings', the Jew seems in modern times to have been trailed by three legends about himself: that he wanders because he does – or doesn't – have a homeland; that he didn't accept Jesus, who went on to be the idol of the West, as a redeemer; and that compared with his contemporaries in the Bible, he has lasted a very long time (you don't meet many Hittites in European cities). In other words, it is the adaptiveness, the judgement and the endurance of the Jews that has made them fascinating and suspect. Using Slavoj Zizek's work to ground his own conclusions, Pick suggests, along psychoanalytic lines, that 'Jews serve as a kind of "ightning conductor" for unwanted parts of the self and for uncontainable social forces. But they also present a category problem ... they do not have a clear place and their homelessness itself is their defining feature. Jews become the emblem of the unrealisable nature of the idealised, unified human group, of the unachievable idyll of a fully harmonious social order.' From this point of view, it seems that the Jews remind people of what Zizek calls, rather grandly, 'the structural impossibility of "society"'.

In the projection theory of anti-semitism that Pick endorses, the Jews are at once a repository and a mirror, a disturbing cartoon of what Victorian and Fin de Siècle England feared about itself. 'The internal negativity of society itself', Pick writes, 'is channelled into the Jew.' The implication is that the projectors are catastrophically unclear about their own values – is it good or bad to have a homeland, to be interested in money, to seek power and influence and sexual satisfaction – and want to foreclose on their own questions and conflicts by producing a scapegoat as an answer. But the drawback of all projection theories – apart from their claim that the unacceptable in ourselves is both representable and potentially knowable – is that they can underestimate the role or agency of the recipients of the projection. It may be glib to say that the Jew and the anti-semite are complicit, but there is no doubt that they are doing something to each other. In other words, if we want to avoid falling into the language of victims and victimisers, it may be more productive to acknowledge, as many psycho-analysts do now, that projection is often a relationship of considerable subtlety. From this point of view, people can be usefully described as being in some sense chosen to be projected into, and as more available to be the recipients of certain projections, by virtue of their own histories and temperaments. People, and groups of people, call up different things in each other – as hypnosis itself disclosed, the range of what is evoked can be bewildering – and this changes over time. *Svengali's Web* suggests that the image of the Jew as ambivalent subject and object has been unusually durable.

The hypnotist removes inhibition, and releases talent, but in doing this he enslaves a person to his will – an extreme description of what every parent, teacher, doctor and political leader does (and knows he does). *Svengali's Web* inevitably leads us to wonder whether hypnosis makes a mockery of our ideas of freedom, or whether seducing and being seduced is actually all we are free to do. There could be worse fates.

Isherwood

Isherwood was a novelist with the inclinations of an autobiographer. There are always characters in his novels who love what he calls 'playacting', who charm and flirt and reinvent themselves whenever necessary, and as much as possible. They are such compelling and irreverent story-tellers that they help us forget about truth-telling; they make everyone, including themselves, feel that it would be earnest and silly to start worrying again about honesty and good behaviour. But they keep coming up against more sincere, serious, passionate types who they are rather troubled by; or, as Isherwood sometimes intimates, who they are not troubled enough by. What makes him more of an experimental writer than he at first seems is that he treats this drama of the opportune and the principled, of the amused and the committed, very self-consciously – as a question of form. So autobiography is a problem in his novels, akin to a conscience. It tempers self-invention with other considerations; and the temptations in story-telling – what he called 'the difficulty of being frank without being indiscreet', the eagerness to tell things for effect – become dramas in themselves. The embarrassment of the narrators in his fiction interests him as much as their confidence or their fluency. What is wonderful about Isherwood is that he wants, if possible, to be delighted by himself.

At the same time there is outrage in his autobiographical writing – of which the *Diaries* and now *Lost Years* are

Review of Christopher Isherwood, *Lost Years: A Memoir 1945–51*,
ed. Katherine Bucknall (Chatto and Windus, 2000),
from the *London Review of Books*

fascinating evidence – about having to be embarrassed about anything. The unusual thing about Isherwood as an autobiographer is that he is never impressed by shame. He doesn't assume that being ashamed of ourselves in public is the best kind of truth-telling. Because he knows so much about charm (and its discontents) – because he is so attentive to the ways in which people go around impressing each other and themselves – he never goes in for the brash boastfulness of modern self-disclosure. His writing, in other words, is an experiment in non-confessional honesty; and *Lost Years* is an intriguing document of a work in progress. In the later autobiographical writings his project was, I think, to write truthfully about himself without feeling that he was submitting to anything (or anyone) by doing so. And on occasion this involved a kind of camp bravado, a sense of being scandalised at there being anything to be scandalised about. But he is never a portentous writer, just an eccentrically curious one, for whom all forms of special pleading, including his own – and *Lost Years* is, among other things, a portrait of the artist as special pleader – are merely refusals to play the game. He has, that is to say, the sulker's inside knowledge about the vanity of sulking. 'Christopher', he writes, looking back at himself in the third person (and almost as a third party),

had always been a model employee. He despised amateurs like Brecht who, when they condescended to work at a film studio, whined and sneered and called themselves whores or slaves. Christopher prided himself on his adaptability. Writing a movie was a game, and each game had a different set of rules. Having learned the rules, Christopher could play along with enjoyment.

Yet as Isherwood and the Christopher of *Lost Years* know, it is not always clear whether learning the rules is a matter of competence or compliance – part of the pleasure of mastery is the submission it entails. As Christopher learns the game of writing for the movies in Hollywood, and learns to write his own kind of fiction, and learns, above all, to play out his sexuality, he is also trying to invent his own games, to discover his very own rules, whatever people might call him as a consequence. 'Wystan was much more mature than Christopher,' he writes in *Christopher and His Kind*. 'Labels didn't scare him.' This is a subtle definition of maturity because it knows so much about intimidation. A lot of Isherwood's characters find themselves jousting at labels. In *Lost Years*, written between the rather dour memoir of his parents, *Kathleen and Frank* (completed in 1970), and his great book *Christopher and His Kind* (published in 1976), Isherwood attempts a stark reconstruction of his early years in California. He is writing in the 1970s about his experience in the late 1940s of being, among other things, a gay man and an aspiring writer. And so he is remembering the old labels in the light of the new ones. And he is writing a memoir that is neither a diary nor a deliberately fictional-ised autobiography. *Lost Years*, Katherine Bucknell tells us in her useful introduction, is part of 'a major new phase – roughly the final third of his career – in which Isherwood moved away from semi-fictionalised writing towards pure autobiography'. 'Pure autobiography' is obviously an odd phrase; and *Lost Years* is more about what, if anything, such a phrase might mean.

Wondering what to write next after finishing *Kathleen and Frank* – having done his parents, so to speak – Isherwood considered writing a book about his spiritual teacher, Swami Prabhavananda, an adult he had been able to take rather more seriously as a guide to living his life. But it was clear to him, as he noted in his diary at the time, that it would be about the fact that his 'personal approach to

Vedanta was, among other things, the approach of a homosexual looking for a religion which will accept him'. So instead of the book he would eventually write as *My Guru and His Disciple* (1980), Isherwood decided that he would write, largely for himself, a kind of 'reconstructed diary' about his sexual life in those apparently lost years in America. It would be, he wrote, 'quite largely a sexual record and so indiscreet as to be unpublishable. It might keep me amused, like knitting, but I should be getting on with something else.' It was not clear exactly what a sexual record might be a record of. Or what kind of person the narrator as the recorder of these experiences would turn out to be. As a schoolboy Isherwood had written an essay entitled 'Omission Is the Beginning of All Art'. *Lost Years* was to be a book in a wholly reputable modern genre: a book about what would otherwise be omitted. But written, at least in the first instance, only for the author. 'Isherwood's "knitting",' Brucknel remarks, 'somewhat like the flow of unselfconscious, free-associative talk in psychoanalysis, evidently set his mind free to delve more directly than ever before into his private life. The very insignificance and confidentiality of the task opened new avenues to self-reflection.' For a writer so fascinated by the performing self to narrow down the audience in this way – to discover what kind of audience he was (or gave) to himself – might well have seemed like a necessary experiment. Isherwood is always at his best when he is showing us how self-consciousness tends to turn up at precisely those moments when we least expect it. Indeed, that we may be most archly self-conscious when we are apparently most forgetful of ourselves. It was his fear that self-consciousness went all the way down – that unselfconsciousness is something we enact, like everything else – that drew Isherwood to Eastern religion, and to writing. The knitting of *Lost Years* stages a more direct delving into the self. And it is as an enquiry – or even as a draft of an enquiry – into the art of self-exposure that it should be read.

When it came to writing, self-consciousness for Isherwood meant that there was pressure to be seen to be something – to be someone in particular, a certain kind of character – in one's description of things. So he would be disconcerted when anything interrupted the preferred performances of his writing self. He observed in his diary around the time he was writing *Lost Years*:

The main thing I have to offer as a writer are my reactions to experience (these ARE my fiction or my poetry, or whatever you want to call it). Now, these reactions are more positive when I am reacting to actual experiences, than when I am reacting to imagined experiences. Yet, the actuality of the experiences does bother me, the brute facts keep tripping me up, I keep wanting to rearrange and alter the facts so as to relate them more dramatically to my reactions.

To be a certain kind of writer, you need certain kinds of fact to react to. Altered or rearranged facts bring out the best in Isherwood. There has to be something out there to react to, but it mustn't be too much of an obstacle. *Lost Years* is an experiment in trying to write (at least a bit) against the grain: he will record the brute facts unaltered, without tripping up.

Isherwood starts from the assumption, or rather tries out the idea, that a 'sexual record' of this period of his life suits the brute-facts approach. Or at least that brute facts are required in any account of sexual life that isn't pointlessly disingenuous. So the fact that several reviewers of this book have tripped up on some of its brute facts – the unsanctimonious sex, the occasional anti-semitism, the bits of spite – is not entirely surprising. It is not news that we are not as nice as we should be (though what we make of this is sometimes news). But Isherwood is not trying to shock himself: he is seeing what happens – how the sentences come out – when he aims not to rearrange the facts. Not the self stripped of its adjectives, but a documentary about a performing self. 'I am writing this', Isherwood begins, 'to clarify my project to myself, not actually to begin work on it ... Because the "I" of this period is twenty years out of date, I shall write about him in the third person ... this helps me to overcome my inhibitions, avoid self-excuses and regard my past behaviour more objectively.' That inhibition and self-excuse more or less sum up the modern sense of self, that the modern, literary 'I' is always felt to be elsewhere, out of date, in the third person, wishing for objectivity, etc., is not a mission statement for Isherwood: it is simply the precondition for writing this particular book. The persistent modern project of trying to set the sexual record straight, and not so straight, has to be about the relationship between inhibition and self-excuse.

It is, of course, easier to talk about inhibition and self-excuse – about one's ideal self and one's alibis – if one talks about the unconscious. But for Isherwood this is part of the problem rather than any kind of solution:

Christopher had – and I still have – a deep-seated reluctance to try tinkering with his own psychological mechanism ... Nowadays, I would say I believe that the unconscious must by its nature remain unconscious. It doesn't belong to me ... All attempts to meddle with it are therefore attempts to impose my will and my ideas of what is good for me upon the infinitely greater wisdom of the non-self.

Lost Years is acutely conscious of the way Christopher imposes his will and idea on others ('Christopher, that shameless flatterer'). But in writing this particular book he is much more attentive to the ways in which he imposes his will and his ideas on himself. As he reconstructs his past he describes his earlier self as virtually obsessed by self-characterisation; and then, every so often, as strangely guilty as he catches himself in the act. Isherwood quotes a 'coldly contemptuous' remark about himself from Keith Vaughan's *Journal and Drawings* in which Vaughan describes Christopher as 'enormously interested in the super-ficialities of life'. And it is as though by quoting this he is reminding himself of something, trying not to keep certain questions about himself at bay. Because if *Lost Years* is perplexed about anything it is about what the super-ficialities of life are and about the things one finds enormously interesting, as opposed to all those things one is supposed to find of such moment. When he writes, for example, of *The Unquiet Grave* that it is Cyril Connolly's 'most maddening and snobbish book, and for that very reason his most fascinating and self-revealing', he is remarking that the self is not revealed in its most (obviously) self-revealing places. What Christopher is enormously interested in in *Lost Years* is sex and, in a rather different sense, in what goes on between people. But he is uncertain – and this is part of the book's subtle amusement – what, if anything, his sexuality reveals about himself.

As a 'confirmed self-preserver' who 'in his inmost heart ... thought of himself as an art-aristocrat or brahmin, a person privileged by his talent to demand the service (he preferred to call it "the co-operation") of others', Christopher is, as he notices, fairly well preserved from being too drastically changed by experience. *Lost Years* recreates a Christopher poised between a quest (and therefore the acknowledgement of some discontent) and a sense that the quest – which takes a more or less religious form – may itself be a distraction, that what Christopher most wants to be is what he already is: gay and a writer of considerable ambition and talent. It is a choice – though Isherwood does not present it in these terms – between the unmaking of the (familiar) self and making the self up, between a disciplined anonymity and being a character.

In so far as *Lost Years* tells a story – it is, of course, integral to Isherwood's project that the book is unplotted, just strung-together anecdotes about what he remembers doing – it is about Isherwood's sexual preferences beginning to come adrift from his spiritual commitments. Not wishing to 'fool everyone into thinking him a saint', Isherwood leaves the Vedanta Center, the religious community that had been his home, with a clear sense, at least in retrospect, of what he was up to:

Should he have left the Center much sooner than he did? Looking back, I find that I can't say yes. It now seems to me that Christopher's embarrassment and guilt feelings were of little importance and his 'spiritual struggles' trivial. What mattered was that he was getting exposure to Swami, that his relations with Swami continued to be (fairly) frank, and that he never ceased to be aware of Swami's love. That he kept slipping away to see Bill Harris wasn't really so dreadful.

What Isherwood catches so well here – and throughout the book – is the self-importance of the present moment; the possibility that our immersion in our lives as we live them – our 'spiritual struggles' – is an inevitable distraction from so many points of view. If it is only in retrospect that we can avoid being so narrow-minded about ourselves, even see that narrow-minded is just what we have been, then recollection, Isherwood intimates, may be the best cure for egotism. What was once a melodrama of moral absolutes becomes a world in which being '(fairly) frank' is fair enough. We may look better if we rearrange the facts, but rearranging the facts is also moral propaganda. Christopher did feel guilt, embarrassment, dread, spiritual struggle then: what Isherwood now sees is an intense sexual and spiritual pragmatism at work. Christopher, he now recognises, boasted of his suffering as a cover-story for his real preferences. *Lost Years* is exhilarating because it is Isherwood's attempt to discover what mattered: not why it mattered to him, but that it mattered. And what is so artful about the writing in this book is that Isherwood's explanations of his own behaviour sound simply like descriptions. It is as though he is saying: this is what Christopher was like, but with none of the usual moral invitations to the reader. Modern self-disclosure is always a provocation: it asks us to assess the self, to judge if we dare. *Lost Years* is more like autobiography as natural history. If there is no point in talking about what a mollusc should be like, why describe what a person should be like?

But erotic life is a big problem for natural history. The main drama of *Lost Years* is the young Isherwood's love affair with a man called Caskey, and the various sexual affairs and encounters that go on around it. What is most striking about the way Isherwood, in being as fairly frank and straightforward as possible, describes their differences is that they sound like perfect opposites. By refusing to be 'novelistic' the characters seem to revert to allegorical type. Christopher appears to be eminently sensible (even about his promiscuity), while Caskey 'didn't want his life to be predictable ... He would tidy the house one day, and drunkenly wreck it the next.' Isherwood's account of their relationship is also, unwittingly perhaps, a formulation of a dilemma about writing.

Christopher's reasonableness, the justice of his case, the moderation of his demands upon Caskey were a bit TOO convincing – and
he knew it. Relations between two human beings who are
supposed to love each other – and perhaps actually do, from time
to time – cannot be regulated by a code of rules. The truth is that
Christopher was no more reasonable than Caskey; he merely had a
knack of manoeuvring himself into positions in which he was,
technically, 'in the right' – whereupon Caskey, with his passive
obstinacy, would not only accept the counterposition of being 'in
the wrong' but would proceed to make the wrong as wrong as he
possibly could. He always behaved worst when there was no
conceivable excuse for his behaviour. That was his kind of integrity.

In Isherwood's view Christopher is often up to his old tricks;
and Christopher's trick is in any given situation to privilege
his own position. (By the same token, much of Isherwood's
fiction is a critique of the self-justifying voice.) Christopher
has the knack of being very impressed by himself; and *Lost
Years* is heartening because Isherwood is more than willing
to be charmed by this, and also to enjoy seeing through it
(ruthless unmasking would be just another knack of the self-
important). To suggest that there were two kinds of integrity
in play here, and not merely two wilful egotisms, is to
suggest that integrity comes in a variety of forms, and that
one of its functions is violent defensiveness. It is as though in
writing *Lost Years* Isherwood was thinking about how to be
as unself-protective a writer as possible without losing his
sense of humour or, indeed, his pleasure as a novelist in
people's self-protectiveness, their flair for self-assurance. He
has a great eye for vanity because his suspicion of it is part of
his relish for it.

Isherwood wrote *Lost Years* in a spirit of generous
suspicion about his younger self. Though there are sudden
(and shocking) moments of self-loathing in the book, he is
not keen to be lured into the refuge of self-criticism. As

though to take against his former self would be a tactless self-betrayal. 'I have no right to sneer at Christopher's soul-searchings', he writes in parenthesis, 'just because they were conducted amidst bottles and boys – but they do embarrass me.' That one's former self has rights, that there should be no privileged position from which to judge one's future or ex-selves, doesn't prevent embarrassment, or the regret at feeling it. That one could (or should) feel embarrassed about one's embarrassment – that shame might be trivial (to use one of Isherwood's key words) in the larger scale of things – is the version of moral progress that Isherwood was after. The terror of being judged, and the ruses of character required to avoid complicity with the more severely demeaning forms it can take, is everywhere in the stark and amused soul-searching of *Lost Years*. And the only authority that is affectionately embraced in the book is E. M. Forster.

Christopher was still a little in awe of him. Not because he thought of Forster as a great writer and as his particular master – he did, but this didn't make him uneasy in Forster's presence; Christopher, who spent so much of his life playing the teacher, found it pleasant and relaxing to become a disciple, now and then. It was as a human being that Forster awed him. Forster demanded truth in all his relationships; underneath his charming un-alarming exterior he was a stern moralist and his mild babylike eyes looked deep into you. Their glance made Christopher feel false and tricky. Christopher reacted to this feeling by trying to make Forster laugh. He usually could; the uneasier he felt, the more sparkling his comedy act became.

This is one of the most interesting double-acts in the book – *Lost Years* continually stages what-Christopher-was-like in the presence of certain significant (and not so significant) others – and one Isherwood redescribes in *Christopher and His Kind*. The truthfulness that makes Christopher feel 'false and tricky'; and the comedy act he uses to manage his unease is where Christopher – and in a different sense, where Isherwood as a writer – is more interestingly poised. Forster's demand for truth is, in Isherwood's canny way, treated as sceptically as Christopher's performing self. As though Isherwood knows that the fool is not less trustworthy than his master. Forster is alarming and stern in the guise of a mild baby: Christopher is amusing and sparkles under the guise of a disciple. And in *Christopher and His Kind* it is the baby Forster that Isherwood goes on about:

He had a baby's vulnerability, which is also the invulnerability of a creature whom one dare not harm. He seemed to be swaddled baby-like, in his ill-fitting suit rather than wearing it ... a friend who was present at the last meeting between them made the comment: 'Mr Forster laughs at you as if you were the village idiot.'

Forster's vulnerability is as much a protection racket, and as integral to who he is, as Christopher's comedy act. To be false and tricky and to sparkle under certain kinds of pressure is as much part of Christopher's truthfulness as being a morally insidious baby is part of Forster's truthfulness. Isherwood as a writer wants to resist the lure of morally privileged positions, while acknowledging the interest of their power. If Christopher had become a stern and alarming moralist in Forster's presence his own truth could not have been told. In other words, what Forster's moral pressure made Christopher feel and do interests Isherwood as much as, if not more than, Forster's principles. To have been more serious with Forster would have been a self-betrayal; and, not incidentally, it would have deprived Forster of his obvious pleasure in Isherwood's company. The master is glum and self-obsessed without his fool.

'And yet', Isherwood writes towards the end of this compelling memoir, 'Christopher *was* open to interference –

by the right person.' 'Interference' is the right word for those, like Christopher, who are so set in their ways; who underneath all the reckless mischief and spiritual struggle, are going their own way. You never feel, reading *Lost Years*, that Christopher won't come through, because he keeps coming across the right person. And he knows that there are plenty of them. And that they are going to be right for different reasons and for different things. And not right for ever.

Mr Phillips

The name is ordinary, so the book announces itself as a book about no one special; though, of course, when men without qualities become the subjects of novels a certain gravity (if not grace) is conferred on them. But even though *Mr Phillips* is really a book about its title – and about what names entitle people to – the title has to be read in the light of the book's epigraph. Taken from Simone Weil's *The Need for Roots*, it plays off, as epigraphs must, the title of the novel against the title that is the source of the quotation: 'Mr Phillips and the Need for Roots'. Tarquin Winot, the now infamous narrator of Lanchester's previous novel, *The Debt to Pleasure*, would have enjoyed the portentous solemnity of the eigraph itself: 'A man left alone in the universe would have no rights whatsoever, but he would have obligations.' Victor Phillips, the eponymous hero of Lanchester's new novel, doesn't think of himself as a man of big themes, and so wouldn't be drawn either to reading about them, or indeed to mocking them. Whether or not *Mr Phillips* would have been Simone Weil's cup of tea – the novel, that is, the character certainly wouldn't have been – her line is there as a guide-line, ushering you into the novel once you've got past the title. And *Mr Phillips* is not demanding as titles go; and as novels go it is exceptionally funny and often astoundingly intelligent – but it is quizzical.

To give a book a person's name inevitably makes you wonder what else the book might be about. Some names, for

Review of John Lanchester, *Mr Phillips* (Faber, 2000), from the *London Review of Books* example, seem to have more roots than others. When Joyce wrote *Ulysses* – another ambitious novel, like *Mr Phillips*, about a day in a man's life: another novel about the way time employs people, whether they are employed or not – he didn't call it 'Bloom' (or 'The Blooms'). Or 'Dedalus'. He needed his novel to have certain kinds of roots, and to give his readers some way into it. As a name, 'Mr Phillips' isn't obviously up to much. But the preoccupations so explicitly stated in the epigraph give Lanchester's novel a genealogy unusual in contemporary British fiction. Solitude and anonymity, the relationship between rights and obligations (i.e., ideas about freedom) were after all the essential issues of the extraordinary, but now unfashionable, Existentialist novels of Sartre and Camus. Despite the echoes of Evelyn Waugh, of Beckett, of Larkin and Alan Bennett, these seem to me to be the real precursors of *Mr Phillips*. Lanchester's new novel, in other words, is that hitherto unthinkable, almost absurd thing, a great English Existentialist novel. Nostalgic rather than loathing of Englishness, as *The Debt to Pleasure* was, *Mr Phillips* is a genuine contemporary philosophical novel, a comedy of manners of thought.

Mr Phillips lives in the strange (and often hilarious) logic of his own thought processes, and most of the novel is an account of a day in his thinking, of how he does it and where it takes him, as he drifts through his first day of unemployment in London, having apparently gone to work as normal. As he is – or was – an accountant, he is wearing a work suit and carrying his briefcase; but he can't actually go to work because he has no work to go to. What occupies him is accounting for his day, observing what is going on around him and drawing his own conclusions. It is a mixture of anthropology and skiving, because he's never seen a day like this before. He has chosen not to tell his wife or his two sons that he has been sacked, and is wandering (and wondering) round Central London until it is, or would have been, time to go home. His day is shadowed by the day he would have been having at work. He is redundant, middle-aged and, for quite a lot of the novel, consumed by sexual fantasies. Even by his own reckoning, he is an ordinary man but, the novel keeps wondering, ordinary compared to what? The plot of this novel about a man who has lost the plot is simply a series of incidents, of encounters – with pornographers, tramps, bank robbers – whom he comes across in his new-found quest to fill up the day. The people he meets and the scenes he witnesses in his new-fangled but now common pilgrimage through a day without a job are every bit as peculiar as the thoughts that pass through his mind. Lanchester writes a kind of magical realism for Little England; the surrealism of the external world Mr Phillips travels through is barely distinguishable from the logical oddities of his internal world. Like Sartre's Existentialist heroes of which he is a mock-heroic version, Mr Phillips is redundant Cartesian man; he thinks strangely and therefore he is. What are people other than their thinking, the novel also seems to wonder. It is the artfulness of *Mr Phillips* that such things are intimated – the book is full of quotidian signs and wonders – but not part of a programme. Unlike Tarquin Winot, Mr Phillips doesn't seem to be suffering from the writer's ideas.

Lanchester is interested in what would once have been called Mr Phillips's imagination: those insistent preoccupations that Mr Phillips wouldn't have the courage or even the wish to tell other people about; all those unofficial things and people that absorb his attention. But it is the way Lanchester represents Mr Phillips's thoughts – the way the stream of consciousness becomes a stream of punctuated words on the page – and the uncanny ease with which we slip into Mr Phillips's mind, that make the novel so remarkable. It is, after all, an effect of style to make this living in someone else's mind seem so natural, given that it is something we never, in actuality, do. As the novel progresses – that is, tracks Mr Phillips from his leaving home in the morning to his return in the evening – 'Mr Phillips' seems less and less the name of a character, in the traditional sense, and more a name for certain ways of thinking, as though the novel is saying: these are the things that pass through us that our names are meant to cover. And Mr Phillips himself shares with the novel's narrator – the transitions between the narrator and Mr Phillips have a subtle and seamless fluency – an obsession with what might be going on in other people's minds:

Mr Phillips had always been impressed by the way conductors used to know exactly who had got on and off and who hadn't paid their fare, as if they had a constantly updated map of the bus in their heads. On the occasions he tried to sit still and not admit to not having paid he always found a conductor hovering at his shoulder demanding the fare. Perhaps they were trained to detect guilty body language. If a bus conductor's wife cheated on him he would know within seconds of getting home.

Like every guilty person Mr Phillips veers between believing that he is opaque and that he is transparent. What he has got to hide – his unemployment, his sexual fantasies, his small meannesses and delinquencies – is most of what he has got to think about. He is the anonymous double of his fantasies. In his little experiment on the bus he is trying to find out whether it's possible to have a secret life. And yet what his alter ego, the narrator, keeps intimating is that he only has a secret life, a life that is secret to him – the life of his own mind.

There are certain things we have to lose our place (our job) to see. So when Mr Phillips remembers going to see a play with his son about another recently unemployed man, King Lear, his response is predictable (the kind of thing you find in Larkin's letters), but (also like the man in Larkin's letters) subtle in refusing the available subtleties, and distrustful of them.

In retrospect he sees it as one of the longest four hours in his life, uncannily similar, in the sensation of discomfort, anxiety and pure duration, to that of waiting in Casualty.

'What did you think?' he risked asking Martin afterwards, on the way back to the car-park ...

'It was long,' said Martin. 'It's always long.'

'I felt sorry for the man who had to take all his clothes off,' said Mr Phillips.

'Edgar,' said Martin. 'Small cock, too.'

'Casualty,' with a capital letter, is as good a name as any for *King Lear*; and one can't help feeling sorry for the man who has to take his clothes off. Mr Phillips's question, in this book that is full of questions and questioning, is the usual one, which is always a bit risky, but that we keep asking. And Martin's answer – 'it's always long' – in its own irrefutable logic, seems, unsurprisingly perhaps, to have picked up what his father was thinking.

Questions come thick and fast to Mr Phillips because, as a modern man, he is nearly always in a need-to-know situation; but his curiosity has become a substitute for his courage, so the only person he can usually ask is himself, who by definition doesn't have the answers. When he's bursting with curiosity he has to keep it to himself:

Take Aids, for one thing ... The porn stars don't look or act as if they have given it a thought, but then they wouldn't, would they? And then having to get erections on demand: is there a knack to it or is it a skill you are born with? And if you got an erection on demand did it feel like a normal erection – did you want to do the same things with it – or was it more somehow impersonal, an indifferent appendage for tool-using purposes, like mankind's famous opposable thumb? And then what would you do about normal sex, would that be distinguishable from work?

In this exhausting and exhaustive double-act for one that is Mr Phillips's internal drama, every point is a good one, and every question is to the point. Mr Phillips is as scrupulously thoughtful about the issue as he can be. You can imagine him as a child wanting to be able to work everything out for himself with that agitated attention to detail that makes one problem lead to another. 'Mr Phillips knows that he will never know,' the narrator comments ruefully; and it is poignant (and apt) that we have to be told this by someone else, as though Mr Phillips is trapped in his perplexity, and trapped by the knowledge that he is trapped. The chatty enthusiasm of his conversation with himself, its eager earnestness and its popular science, give us a glimpse of the way he keeps himself company. Because of the way he has befriended himself you can't imagine Mr Phillips having a best friend. He is like a man who has left himself alone in the universe.

One way of not feeling quite so alone in the universe is to be superstitious. The feeling that there are other powers, whether malign or in some way on our side, makes life seem more like something going on inside a novel than the random, intractable thing that we have to go through un-assisted. Whenever logic breaks down in Mr Phillips's endless enquiry into how things work, superstition turns up; however rational the enquiry, reason is liable to create the madness it is trying to avert. Getting into a lift Mr Phillips is thrown into what he would never call the phenomenology of mind:

Covertly inspecting the overhead display Mr Phillips can see that the 14th floor is actually the 13th, and that the number has been changed as a concession to superstition. This is something that he has never been able to work out. If you thought there was something dangerous about the number 13, surely the 13th floor would be dangerous whatever you called it, since it is the fact of 13 and not the word that is the problem. It was treating the gods or the fates or God himself – not that this was the sort of thing you would expect Him to bother about – as if He was very stupid to think that they or He wouldn't notice.

As Mr Phillips notes with slight embarrassment ('covertly'), no one is fooled, not even the authorities, if you just change the names. But proving the madness of this double-think sounds as mad as the thing itself. What kind of world is it that gives us questions and answers like this, and what are we like if this is how we find ourselves thinking? And the answer in *Mr Phillips* is that the world is frightening and we are embarrassed.

Mr Phillips is an acute observer of the way people guarantee failure by the manner in which they pursue success. The trains, for example, must run on time if everything, especially work, is going to work. 'The platform will close thirty seconds before departure because that way more people miss the train.' The departure time should not be called the departure time, any more than the 14th floor should be so misnamed. But our solutions embroil us in our problems. 'In Mr Phillips's experience so many people avoid the nearest carriage on the assumption that it will be the most full, and instead get into the next carriage along, or even the next but one, that it is often those carriages which are the fullest whereas the nearest carriage is in fact, relatively speaking, reasonably empty.' Whatever Mr Phillips does, he always makes good sense. But his plain, well-qualified reasonableness ('relatively speaking, reasonably empty'), his persuasive practical intelligence, is of a piece with the world he describes. If everybody follows Mr Phillips's suggestion about how to find a reasonably empty carriage, the same problem will reproduce itself. The great failing is to fear failure, and once it starts it never stops. Mr Phillips's quest for truth – and *Mr Phillips* is such a moving book because Mr Phillips is never patronised by his author – is complicated by his quest for 'relative' comfort and convenience. What is so disturbing about the world for Mr Phillips is that it is so difficult to outwit it, yet that is what he believes he needs to do. The way to solve the problems he sees in life is to think them through, but then the thinking in its turn becomes the problem.

If his 'diseased intellect' makes Mr Phillips the kind of modern man D. H. Lawrence wanted to abolish – and makes D. H. Lawrence one of the phantom reviewers of the book – it is his very real shyness, his taken-for-granted embarrassments that make him so winning. He assumes, without boasting, an ordinary vulnerability for himself; and that means that his small-scale heroism (going into a porn shop in Soho), and his more ambitious feats (confronting bank robbers), are moments when he defies something powerful in himself. Shyness has rather a bad press among the more glibly suspicious – among, that is, the psychologically-minded – because the ways in which shyness seeks and controls attention are always more vivid than whatever else the shy are so privately struggling with. Lanchester is a great writer about shyness – and indeed about many of the other awkwardnesses of everyday life – because he is so alert to the fact that the drama in people's lives often consists precisely of all those ways they have of minimising the drama. And the spectacle of a certain kind of Englishness is the spectacle of people avoiding making a spectacle of themselves. Mr Phillips does this – and, in this, is not unlike a novelist – by describing what he does in a very particular way. Like the accountant that he is (or was), he lists and counts and clarifies. He turns the hot, frantic opera of his fantasy life into a prosaic documentary. The knowingness of the narrator – the fact that Mr Phillips is somehow close to his heart, but that he can be wittier, more deadpan than Mr Phillips knows himself to be – exposes Mr Phillips as an absurd hero, but not a ridiculous man:

Mr Phillips takes his courage in his hands and crosses the street, pushes through the curtain and goes into the sex shop. It is a square box of a room with magazines on two walls, a display cabinet on the third and a counter on the fourth. There are two other customers, both men, and a bored, grumpy fat man at the till. Both of the men are leafing through the magazines with a flushed listlessness.

As the scene develops he becomes more paralysed and self-absorbed, a voyeur of the voyeurs, attending to the signs, but unable to go the whole way. 'A large sign over the magazine rack says "Try Before You Buy is NOT Our Policy". Mr Phillips feels too shy to actually pick up any of the magazines so he merely stands and looks at the covers.' Lanchester writes with such canny, unobtrusive accuracy – 'merely' and 'actually' are so close to the bone here – that every scene in the book seems to be wholly ordinary and unexceptional, and yet emblematic of what we imagine to be Mr Phillips's entire life. As the narrator's voice blends into the 'voice' of Mr Phillips's thoughts, we see Mr Phillips bringing the scene under control. If he was less shy, we are led to believe, he might have picked up one of the magazines, but not necessarily looked at it. For Mr Phillips, description is an attempt at slow-motion; excess is the disorder of the day.

When Mr Phillips is not estimating probabilities – when and how he might die, say, or remembering the troubling relationship between the odds of winning the lottery and the odds of dying on any given day – he is making lists. He has so much material to organise, and even more now that he is out and about during the day. Once he is out, for example, he realises how many places in London he's never been to: 'Kew Gardens or Hampton Court or Teddington Lock or the Royal Opera House or the Barbican . . .' (This is one of the shorter lists in the novel: there are only 12 places.) But in his wish for accurate records there is always a muted yet mounting hysteria, as though once this sensible rage for order is unleashed it could turn into pure rage:

Mr Phillips must have witnessed many thousands of violent incidents, shootings and explosions and stabbings and abductions and rapes and fist-fights and drive-by machine-gunnings, and assassination-style head shots and Saturday Night Special shootings, and cars blown up by shoulder-fired rocket-launchers, and rooms systematically cleared by grenades followed by machine-gun fire, and petrol stations blown up by deliberately dropped cigarette lighters, but all of these were on television (or occasionally at the movies).

This could not be more straightforward as an account. Though what it is an account of, this singular sentence with its reassuring clarification tacked onto the end like a moral, is not clear. It is Mr Phillips's art, and the artfulness of *Mr Phillips*, to make many strange things sound self-evidently true and unself-evidently mad. The God that is in these details is too careful about something.

Rather like his questions, Mr Phillips's lists – of which there are many hilarious and horrifying examples – always threaten to get out of hand and go on for ever (one thing always leads to another). And it is his sense of an endlessness, of something in him that he cannot put a stop to, that is the informing terror of the book. But his rationalising of things keeps being interrupted by unexpected memories. In Mr Phillips's accounts of himself as a father to his sons, and as a son to his father, the novel is more starkly moving; poignancy is Lanchester's secret pleasure in this book. It is not merely that Mr Phillips comes to life when he can't account for things, but that he comes to a different kind of life (Lanchester doesn't pit the rational against the irrational, but the irrational against itself). Indeed, when it comes to memory, the vices of Mr Phillips's plain style – his aversion to melodrama, to stylishness – become a remarkable virtue. When he happens to remember something, the narrator takes him on his own terms, and the effect is the haunting that can only be created by the haunted:

In childhood, as far as he can remember, crying had inside it the idea that this feeling would go on for ever – that the pain, whatever it was, that was causing you to cry was infinite and would possess you for ever. Or you would live inside it for ever. Now he sees it as the first vague intimation of what death would be like – to be in the same state without end.

Only Mr Phillips would be able to see (and say) that crying had inside it an idea.

When Mr Phillips finds himself, surprisingly, caught up in a bank robbery on his fateful day, he speculates, as he lies face down on the floor, about the conscientiousness of bank robbers; how they need to think of everything. 'There must be a lot of detail to have to think about, being a bank robber,' he muses in his *Alice in Wonderland* way. 'It would seem like a job for the headstrong and reckless but there must be a great deal of planning in it too.' But then, out of nowhere, Mr Phillips has what a policeman calls, after the robbers have been successfully disarmed, 'your bright idea, sir, if you don't mind my putting it like that'. He suddenly stands up, in the middle of the drama, and says: 'I'm not doing that any more.' It is a moment of startling and consummate bravery; by refusing to comply – and it is the being told to lie down that Mr Phillips is objecting to, not just (or necessarily) the robbery – Mr Phillips makes his existential stand. And in the several pages that describe what is going through his mind during the robbery, nothing prepares either the reader or Mr Phillips himself for what he is about to do. It is what would once have been called a pure act of freedom; a risk taken in reckless disregard for the consequences. And of course, as it would in Mr Phillips's world, his break for freedom has its downside because the press who interview him after the robbery threaten to blow his cover. He, too, having had his job stolen, is on the run.

When Eliot wrote of Henry James that 'he had a mind so fine that no idea could violate it,' it was not altogether clear what James's mind would have had to be like for this to be true. Eliot's strange, virginal James seems rather to have had a style – like Lanchester's in *Mr Phillips* – that no idea could violate. But the idea of minds, or indeed styles of writing, being violated by ideas is an interesting one. That people can suffer from ideas, and that writers can be ruined by them, is as much a story about what ideas are supposed to be like, as it is a story about what people are supposed to be like. Novels have always explored the relationship between characters and their beliefs, and the ways in which a character might be something other than his ideas. But there are also, clearly, novels of ideas – like Sartre's or Iris Murdoch's or Coetzee's – in which the novelist more or less knows what he thinks about things (knows what the issues are), and in which discernible ideas, or theories, or positions are deliberately dramatised; in which ideas are used to make the characters vivid, and not the other way around. In the novel of ideas – or its contemporary equivalent, the psychological novel – everything inside a character, everything about a character, has to become an idea, and then to be spoken, and then to be contested. At their worst these novels, like Platonic dialogues, can be dramas of the archest kind of knowingness. They want us to be able to paraphrase them, so that we can go on with the debate; and to know that that is what we are involved in.

In *Mr Phillips* Lanchester has written not a novel of ideas, but a novel about how a person's ideas work inside him, and can seem to be the limits of his world; and not a psychological novel because neither Lanchester nor his narrator affects to have a superior knowledge of their hero. With its virtuosity of style, its lack of casual sentimentality, and its easy way with the comic problems of philosophy, *Mr Phillips* is a contemporary *Tristram Shandy*. A new name as a sign of the times.

Russell

In the introduction to the first volume of his biography of Russell, *Betrand Russell: The Spirit of Solitude*, Ray Monk was clear, as his title indicated, about the story he had to tell, though also daunted by the amount of material he had to work with. The bibliography of Russell's work lists more than three thousand publications, and this doesn't include the letters he wrote – over forty thousand of them. It was, of course, a long life, but even so, as Monk noted, 'the quantity of writing that Russell produced in his lifetime almost defies belief.' Russell may have experienced himself as a ghost: but he was an unusually articulate one. Monk was even more struck by what he called, in a characteristically prudent phrase, Russell's 'detailed self-absorption'. All this, one might think, would be something of a gift to a biographer: a dispersed autobiography to accompany the known facts. And yet in retrospect – in the light of this troubled and troubling second volume – one can see that Monk was uneasy about something. 'A perhaps surprising amount of this vast output', he wrote, 'was concerned with himself.' 'Concerned' as in 'worried', 'preoccupied' and 'baffled'; and 'concerned with himself', as it turns out, because he was quite unable, in Monk's convincing account, to be concerned about anyone else. People become self-absorbed when being absorbed in others has become a problem. And so to be fascinated by the self-absorbed can be an especially lonely (and therefore enraging) task.

Review of Ray Monk, *Bertrand Russell 1921–1970: The Ghost of Madness* (Cape, 2000), from the *London Review of Books*

'To a large extent', Monk wrote in the first volume, the story of the first half of Russell's life is 'the story of those battles to overcome the distance he felt between himself and the rest of the world'. And in his largely sympathetic portrait of these fifty years Monk seemed to join forces with Russell, making him sound at once the poignant victim of a terrible childhood – by the age of three he had lost his mother, his father and his sister – and a man passionately perplexed by the meaning of life. If there was disillusionment everywhere in Russell's life – if he was a person who, out of a benighted, furious innocence, wreaked emotional havoc – it was, Monk intimated, understandable. And to wreak havoc among such distinguished and talented people (the Eliots, the Woolfs, Ottoline Morrell, Wittgenstein, etc.) was an enlivening story, even when it was a dismaying one. Sympathetic, as he obviously was, to his larger-than-life subject, Monk made it all but impossible not to feel for him, not because Russell was a 'genius', but because of what being a genius couldn't help him with. Intelligence, it can sometimes seem, is the last refuge of the emotionally deprived. If you are never given the opportunity to be ordinary, extraordinary is all you can be.

So for Monk, at the outset, it was essential to see Russell's life as an attempt to find answers to 'a single problem: the problem of his acute sense of isolation and loneliness, a problem that was for him compounded by his extraordinarily deep-seated fear of madness'. Russell's bereftness and sense of exclusion, as Monk showed in painful detail, started in early childhood – when there was no hope of making sense of it and all he could do was endure it. It is reductive but probably true to think that his later philosophical quest for really reliable truths had some connection with his childhood experience: he was always wanting something secure on which to base his life. Excessive suffering in childhood often makes people cruel because it makes them unduly self-protective. The self Russell had to invent, quite early on, as a refuge from other people – its callousness, its wit, its stringent scepticism, its emotional evasiveness, its craving for flattery but not for other people, its abstracted version of love – was not, as this book makes abundantly clear, an appealing one. But it was better suited to the brilliant and aristocratic young man of Monk's first volume than to the 'famous philosopher' of later years, who did more and more work that he never really valued. If the story of this second volume is of two bitterly failed marriages, and the acknowledged end of Russell's original contribution to philosophy, and of Russell, in Monk's view, turning into a caricature of the inspiring liberal political idealist he had been (and been for so many people) in his youth, it is also the story of how both Russell and his biographer dealt with their disappointment in him.

Russell seems to have begun to believe in middle age that he had nothing left to offer anyone: not a rare experience, but one's own case must always feel special. And Russell, after all, had been more than famous both for his extraordinary gifts and for reinventing the idea of the public-spirited philosopher, the genius as public man. Disappointment with other people is easier to deal with, and rather more exhilarating, than disappointment with oneself. If one can bear it, though, disappointment with oneself may lead somewhere: once you realise you've got your ideal self wrong you can come up with a new one. In Monk's view, Russell wasn't able to do this; and vanity became a cover for self-contempt. Instead of discussing things and reconsidering them he postured with half-baked opinions. He became, in short, a caricature of the man of conviction, the uneasy double of the man of strong feeling.

At the same time one of the fascinating aspects of this second volume of what must be one of the most striking biographies of our time – and of the fashions of our times – is watching the biographer lose sympathy with his subject; and, as a sympathetic man, not quite knowing what to replace sympathy with. Monk is perhaps too scrupulous in not thinking about roads not taken, about what Russell might have done. Yet Russell, much more than Wittgenstein, the subject of Monk's previous biography, provides the occasion for speculating about alternative lives within the Life. As it is, his growing dislike of Russell has obliged him to reveal more of himself than he would have wanted to. Biography, after all, is an unusual form of coupledom, in that only one person gets to make the choices. It isn't surprising that there may have to be a certain amount of disentangling.

Perhaps the main reason, Monk writes in his preface,

that this has been a difficult book to write has been my growing realisation of the tragedy of Russell's life ... I do not just mean that there was sadness in Russell's life, though, to be sure, the degree of suffering he endured – and caused – has been one of the hardest revelations of my work on this book ... what I mean when I speak of tragedy is principally that Russell's life seems to have been inexorably drawn towards disaster, determined on its course by two fundamental traits of character: a deep-seated fear of madness and a quite colossal vanity.

Monk is not a rhetorically coercive writer or a sentimental one, but what he is describing here is something like a distasteful ordeal. When 'colossal vanity' is seen as a trait – rather than, say, a forlorn and pernicious self-cure for the fear of madness, for the fear of worthlessness – repulsion

214

has begun to replace the work of explanation. Monk, in other words, doesn't want to be complicit with the things about Russell that appal him; and having come upon something in Russell's character that he calls vanity, with all the history and associations this old-fashioned word brings with it, he implies that understanding may be precisely what isn't called for, even if a certain amount of blame and punishment come in to fill the vacuum. Madness and vanity make rather different demands on a biographer. In the first volume Monk spoke of 'isolation and loneliness' and madness: in this second volume the tables have been turned. The first volume ended with the birth of Russell's first child and the biographer and his subject full of hope. The best, most ordinary redemption seemed to be at hand. 'In their various ways,' Monk wrote,

his early religious beliefs, his belief in the Platonic realm of mathematics, his faith in revolutionary socialism and even the ecstasies of romantic love had all disappointed him ... But fatherhood, the binding love and loyalty (as Conrad put it) between a man and his son – that, surely, was as real as any contact can be between one person and another. And in that contact, equally surely Russell thought, he would find the lasting release from the prison of the self, from the feeling of being a 'ghost', for which he had longed all his life.

Instead of his quest to find ideas and people to believe in (and to believe) Russell might have wondered why his life had been driven by the need to believe. Or, indeed, what kind of experience belief – or 'surety', to use Monk's more alert term – was for him such that he felt it to be the thing most lacking in his life. Ghostliness, the prison of the self, had made some things possible: they suited him for work in analytic philosophy, and they drew him to the counter-life of that philosophical tradition in which love dissolves the scepticism needed to sustain the solitariness of the self. An early commitment to logic, socialism and romantic love had put Russell at the forefront of contemporary life: but after the war the glamorous genius who had been, among so many other things, a hero to the younger generation for his resistance to the war, and especially to conscription, became, as Monk says, 'famous, not for his philosophy, but for his politics'. And Russell's politics sometimes get short shrift in this book because for Monk Russell's political ideas are vitiated by the unscrupulousness of his private life.

Russell's 'best philosophical writing', he writes, 'is subtle, nuanced and unafraid of complexity':

He supports his views with rigorous and sophisticated arguments, and deals with objections carefully and respectfully. In most of the journalism and political writing that he produced in the second half of his life, however, these qualities are absent, replaced with empty rhetoric, blind dogmatism and a cavalier refusal to take the views of his opponents seriously. The gulf in quality between Russell's writings on logic and his writings on politics is cavernous. The question that must be raised, therefore, is why he abandoned a subject of which he was one of the greatest practitioners since Aristotle in favour of one to which he had very little of any value to contribute.

In Monk's view, a certain kind of 'civilised' (i.e., liberal) ideal has been replaced by its opposite – John Stuart Mill has turned into the Ayatollah. if Russell's subtle consideration of disagreement was replaced by vacuous dogmatism, as Monk asserts it was – and everything he quotes in his book supports this contention – it may say as much about the precariousness of these values as it does about Russell's psychological make-up. Indeed, the two are inextricable. It would, on the one hand, be legitimate to ask what the so-called emotional problems of childhood are that certain liberal values might seem to be a solution to. Monk's biography is not psychologically-minded in this way, but there is nevertheless an implication – partly obscured by the inevitable time-lag between the two volumes – that the traumas of Russell's childhood made his attachment to values and people inherently unstable. But one could equally well ask what it is about these values, so impressively represented by the younger Russell, that makes them vulnerable to reversal. What it is about liberalism that makes liberals so prone to self-contempt. The tragedy of the second half of Russell's life, as Monk tells it, is that he tried to devote his life to fatherhood and politics – that is, to persuading people to live in a certain way – and in doing so revealed himself to be an opinionated egotist who would listen to no one, and speak for everyone.

And yet if there is something monstrous about the older Russell – about his chronic insensitivity to the needs of his wives and children, the mercenariness of his lecture tours in America where he is endlessly contemptuous of his audiences, the absurd self-importance of his political positions on the Cold War – he was a strangely evocative presence for those who knew him, and they were likely to be more revealing about him than he was about himself. Or rather, he afforded other people the opportunity to say interesting things that were only apparently about him. 'Bertie', Keynes said, 'held two ludicrously incompatible beliefs: on the one hand, he believed that all the problems of the world stemmed from conducting human affairs in a most irrational way; on the other that the solution was simple, since all we had to do was to behave rationally.' When Virginia Woolf noted in her diary that Russell was 'brilliant of course; perfectly outspoken; familiar ... His adventures with his wives diminish his importance,' she was also saying something about certain connections in her own mind that Russell's conversation had elicited. Wittgenstein's comment, in the same period, about Russell's views on marriage, sex and free love – 'If a person tells me he has been to the worst places I have no right to judge him, but if he tells me it was his superior wisdom that enabled him to go there, then I know he is a fraud' – is startling in its clarity. But all these remarks, and there are many more in the book, show, as Monk suggests, that there was something about Russell's much vaunted (often by himself) intelligence that disturbed people – including his biographer – into correcting him. But also into having their own thoughts about things that were important to them. Russell couldn't quite accept himself as he was, couldn't ever take himself on his own terms. And it was this perhaps that turned the people who knew him well in the second half of his life into devoted fans or obsessive critics.

Monk may not have been a devoted fan, despite the comparison with Aristotle, which is pushing it a bit, but he has turned in this second volume into a persistent critic. He speaks of the 'glibness and wilful shallowness' of Russell's remarks, describes him as 'intellectually careless' and capable of the most 'credulous nonsense', and insists on the 'self-delusion to which Russell was prone whenever he wrote on social, political and historical subjects'. If the tone is often one of amazed outrage – 'Seeking the intellectual roots of Fascism in the adoption of a pragmatist theory of truth seems almost breathtakingly naive and implausible' – it is partly because there is now in Monk an unflagging distrust of Russell's motives reminiscent of D. H. Lawrence's suspicions about him. Or rather a new-found, narrower surety about what was driving him. The young Russell may have been seeking love, truth and justice, but the older Russell is in search of his own importance ('Russell now began to see himself as a world leader in his own right'). What Monk can't stand about the later Russell is the way he is always, whatever else he is supposedly doing, privileging himself, exercising the ghost's need for exceptional visibility. If Monk flaunts Russell's incoherence – and he is sometimes crudely reductive in his account of Russell's political thinking – it is because, like Russell, he seems baffled by his own disappointment. 'Vanity' speaks more of frustration than of explanation.

'A world in which the superiority of the British over the rest of mankind was safely assumed, and the virtues of reason, moderation and aristocratic leisure accorded their proper respect was, one suspects, a world to which Russell yearned to belong,' Monk writes. When the clever, neglected child turns into the snobbish, neglectful adult, it is difficult to take his side. And yet what is remarkable about this book is that Monk's turning against his subject, far from marring the book as it might have, raises its emotional pitch and often heightens its intellectual interest. This is partly because Monk writes in a way, and quotes in a way, that makes it clear that he is not, despite his disappointment, on a fault-finding mission, but rather, in the position of someone who has come upon a kind of scandal, even though scandal is not something he would have chosen, ideally, to have dealt with. He cannot abide the way Russell began now to trade on his 'genius' through the writing of popularisations and pot-boilers – *Why I Am Not a Christian*, *A History of Western Philosophy*, *Unpopular Essays* and so on – and he is notably unimpressed by Russell's supposedly passionate espousal of causes. After the war Russell had 'argued repeatedly and consistently that the abolition of nuclear weapons would be futile', but then in 1958 he was elected president of the Campaign for Nuclear Disarmament. Suddenly, Monk intimates, Russell wants to Ban the Bomb: 'Having formulated this view, Russell characteristically came to regard it as the only view consistent with common sense, and became inclined to think that anyone who rejected it must either lack intelligence or positively want to see the spread of nuclear weapons to all the nations of the world and (therefore) the total destruction of human life.' It is always worth wondering why, at any given moment, changing one's mind is considered to be a vice or a virtue.

But Monk's vehemence about Russell's intellectual opportunism – the eagerness with which he took positions, the ruthlessness of his self-regard – is never merely high-minded or even high-handed. The reason, I think, is that for Monk the scandal (or what he calls the tragedy) of Russell's life lay in his relationship with his children; and Monk, who pointedly dedicates this book to his own children, sees the children, as Russell himself had wanted to do, as the heart of the matter. Russell, it seems, treated his children rather as though they were ideas. Everyone adores their children: it is liking them and living with them every day that is difficult. Russell's solution to the difficulty was to turn them, his first child John especially, into projects; as Monk suggests, his relationships with his children were not dissimilar to the relationships he had to the causes he took up and the beliefs he professed: intransigent, subtly (and not so subtly) domineering, and infinitely rationalised. They were there to reflect him, and to reflect well on him. Russell, as Monk documents in patient and disturbing detail, could only spread the estrangement that he had felt as a boy. Despite his always good (i.e., justified) intentions, Russell left what Monk lists as a catalogue of disasters: 'two embittered ex-wives, an estranged schizophrenic son and three grand-daughters who felt themselves haunted by the ''ghosts of maniacs'', as Russell himself had described his family back in 1893.' Put like this, Russell sounds like the anti-hero of a contemporary (i.e., sanity, madness and the family) gothic horror, in which the transgenerational haunting is un-stoppable, and every life seems ghost-written. 'Especially haunted', Monk writes, was Russell's granddaughter Lucy: 'In the early morning of 11 April 1975, Lucy caught the bus from Porthcurno to Penzance and got off at the village of St Buryan, where she walked into the churchyard, climbed on top of one of the graveyard monuments, poured paraffin over herself and set herself alight.'

Monk doesn't suggest that Russell in any simply malic-ious way caused what happened to his families. Nor does he dignify the story in a House-of-Atreus kind of way. But if as a biographer you are able to avoid the traditional options, what do you do to make the story intelligible? Monk's solution is to be meticulously critical of Russell's writing and as straightforward as possible in the recounting of his family affairs. He never underestimates the terror Russell lived with for most of his life. So, for example, in describing 'quite *how* hard' it was for him to bear the fact of his son John's insanity ('talking to John himself, Russell seemed to assume ... was a waste of time. John was mad, irrational, and there was simply no point in consulting him about anything') he quotes Russell's *Autobiography* as a way into the vexed question. For over sixty years, Russell wrote, he had been 'subject to violent nightmares in which I dream that I am being murdered, usually by a lunatic'; this fear 'caused me, for many years, to avoid all deep emotion and live, as nearly as I could, a life of intellect tempered by flippancy'. There was something about himself that Russell knew he needed to be rid of, but he never knew what it was. By not overplotting the book or overdetermining the connections, <u>Monk makes it plain that it was Russell's personal solution to his own terrors that terrorised his children</u>, just as it was the way in which he estranged himself from the problems of his life that ultimately disabled him. In short, he couldn't bear his children's vulnerability and this made him unusually harsh.

All modern biographies, not to mention modern lives, are hexed by what to do about the childhood. If we are to all intents and purposes morally and emotionally formed when we are morally and emotionally undeveloped – as both Russell and Monk, among others, seem to suggest – then our accounts of childhood become, at worst, an all-purpose alibi and at best, an opportunity to reconsider our moral judgements. Punishing adults for their childhoods is a pernicious form of moral confusion. And Monk works hard to avoid it. To have made this a history-of-ideas biography and not to have bothered with the childhood would have been to collude with Russell's own attempt to think himself too intellectually out of his predicaments. And yet taking Russell's childhood terrors as seriously as Russell himself took them has created an instructive dilemma for his biographer.

With his two biographies, first of Wittgenstein and now of Russell, Monk has changed the way we think about the lives of our most distinguished eccentrics. But no modern biographer quite knows what to do with those other distinguished eccentrics, the children that their subjects once were. Clearly no one has ever been a child in the ways in which childhood is represented. It is the art of biographers to make childhood matter, or to show us again why it doesn't.

Ravelstein

In Diana Trilling's memoir, *The Beginning of the Journey*, she tells a story about Saul Bellow to illustrate the effect that Lionel Trilling had on the people he met. Lionel, she writes,

... always retained a certain air of unassailability. There were people whom this seemed to disturb. In middle life, he lectured at the University of Chicago, and Saul Bellow, who taught there and with whom he had become pleasantly acquainted in the early fifties when Bellow was writing *The Adventures of Augie March*, invited him to have a drink after his talk. For their drinking place Bellow chose a bar in a desperate quarter of the city; it was the gathering place of drunks and deadbeats, a refuge of people who had been irreparably damaged by life. What other explanation of Bellow's choice could there be than the wish to test Lionel's ability to handle himself in such surroundings?

We may know what she means, we may be able to imagine what this bar was like, but her assuming our complicity in this description is, as it were, part of the problem. And it is a problem that Saul Bellow has been unusually alert to in his fiction. It is the problem of culture, and particularly so-called high culture, as a version of pastoral; but a version of pastoral that can be made to look unassailable because of the apparent complexity and subtlety and depth of its inclusions. A strangely modern version of pastoral, because it persuades us to forget that pastoral is what it is. At its worst it is a refuge masquerading as a profound engagement. If, despite Diana Trilling's rhetorical question, this scene seems

Review of Saul Bellow, *Ravelstein* (Viking, 2000), from *Raritan* emblematic in more ways than one – of two antagonistic Jewish (and not only Jewish) aspirations, of the composure of the cultured versus the disarray of what they hide from, of the need to know people by testing them rather than by taking them on their own terms – it is partly because it stages so neatly the preoccupations, the obsessions, of both Trilling and Bellow. The heroes of Bellow's fiction – and the Ravelstein of Bellow's title is no exception – are always wholeheartedly assailable, and, above all, attentive to other people's airs (and often their graces). And they are always men who live, somewhere in themselves, in a desperate quarter; and, are, as everyone is, irreparably damaged by life. But unlike almost everyone else, they are astonishingly articulate, and learned, and poignantly moving and amused about their various predicaments. However abject, they luxuriate in words and things (Humboldt, Bellow wrote, 'spoke wonderfully of the wonderful, abominable rich'). Ravelstein, the great teacher dying of Aids, is in this great tradition of Bellow's grandly destitute, and it is, remarkably, one of Bellow's finest novels.

Trilling is always trying to persuade us (and presumably himself) in his criticism that the culture he values isn't, and shouldn't be, a retreat from anything. And Bellow's fiction, one way or another, has always been about, has always dramatised the romance of culture and learning. For Bellow – for whom the self-made man is essentially the self-educated man – it hasn't been only about connecting the prose and the passion, but more about seeing what the deadbeats and the professors make of each other. As both Trilling and Bellow are sticklers for the noble life – and are keen to tell us what we should be doing to ennoble our lives – they are determinedly stylish about the crude and the vulgar (in this sense Trilling's composure and the brash eloquence of Bellow's heroes are mirror-images of each other). They are, in their quite different ways, both enthralled by, and at their most fascinating about, sophistication.

Writing in *Sincerity and Authenticity* about how the novelists of the nineteenth century were 'anything but confident that the old vision of the noble life could be realized', Trilling refers to Bellow's Moses Herzog:

When, for example, a gifted novelist, Saul Bellow, tries through his Moses Herzog to question the prevailing negation of the old vision and to assert the value of the achieved and successful life, we respond with discomfort and embarrassment. And the more, no doubt, because we discern some discomfort and embarrassment on the part of Mr Bellow himself, arising from his sufficiently accurate apprehension that in controverting the accepted attitude he lays himself open to the terrible charge of philistinism, of being a defector from the ranks of the children of light, a traitor to Spirit. We take it as an affront to our sense of reality that a contemporary should employ that mode of judging the spiritual life which we are willing to accept and even find entrancing when we encounter it in Shakespeare's romances.

As terrible charges go, one might think, there are probably worse ones. And yet, as ever, Trilling has located, in his elegant, Freudian way, a conflict. Or at least some kind of paradoxical tension in Bellow's work. If it is old-fashioned, if not actually regressive, to assert the value of the achieved and successful life, what else can be asserted in its stead? If the 'reconciliations and redemptions' – in a phrase Allan Bloom, the putative original for Ravelstein, uses with reference to Shakespeare's romances – of these romances affronts our contemporary sense of reality, then what forms of disarray are we going to put our money on?

Ravelstein, the political philosopher and worshipper of Eros, has devoted his life to teaching the best that has been thought and done about the ordering of the soul and the ordering of the polis; and he is now dying of Aids. And he has asked his older close friend, a writer called Chick, to write his biography, the final testament to an achieved and successful life. Or rather, the contemporary genre in which the notions of success and achievement are both assumed and put into question. More than any of his other books, *Ravelstein* seems like a wholly successful example of an utterly implausible genre: a contemporary Jewish Platonic dialogue. Like the tricky romance of taking Trilling to that bar – wondering whether it would end in tears, or just what it would end in – Bellow stages a great double-act in this novel to explore the ways in which people are informed, in the most various senses of this word, by the people they love and admire.

It is 'the promise [Chick] had made years ago to write a short description of Ravelstein and to give an account of his life'. And as a kept promise of sorts – the book we read is an account of preparing to write this biography – it is an ironic vindication, against the grain of modern biography, that a short description of somebody, done with sufficient skill, can be an account of their life. Bellow intimates not (quite) that all biographers are failed novelists; but that all biographies are failed or ersatz novels. The novel *Ravelstein*, in other words, is not a biography of someone called Ravelstein, nor of someone called Allan Bloom. It is a fiction about biography; and the much-publicised connections made between Bellow's close friend Bloom and Bellow's (and Chick's) subject Ravelstein are to the point and beside it. They are, as it were, integral to Bellow's sense of, or joke about, biography in this book. Ravelstein, we are told on several occasions, loved listening to classical music played on 'original instruments': and what, we are made to wonder in a book about someone who wonders about virtually everything, does original mean? What is involved in this fantasy of origins? If Ravelstein is 'like' Allan Bloom, or 'based on' Allan Bloom, he is also, unsurprisingly, like Moses Herzog, like Humboldt. And they are all, in their way, originals; original instruments, original voices. People who believe that if you admire something enough you will become the thing you admire.

It is one of Ravelstein's projects to divorce his students – who are always his devoted protégés – from what used to be called their backgrounds. 'He hated his own family and never tired of weaning his gifted students from their families. His students, as I've said, had to be cured of the disastrous misconceptions, the "standardised unrealities" imposed on them by mindless parents.' For Ravelstein, origins and originality are at odds with each other; he persuades his students to disown, as he has done, their supposed histories. But even though Ravelstein is, by definition, no Freudian – and as a committed European no Emersonian either, although Thoreau, as we shall see, puts in some interesting appearances – his biographer-to-be, Chick, as he is aptly named, has a more familiar, literary-Freudian cast of mind. So he reads Ravelstein in a way Ravelstein would never read himself; that is, through a particular canon of literary allusions. 'His lot, his crew, his disciples, his clones who dressed as he did, smoked the same Marlboros, and found in these entertainments a common ground between the fan clubs of childhood and the Promised Land of the intellect towards which Ravelstein, their Moses and their Socrates led them.' Bellow has always been able to pack a sentence; and at its worst this can give his writing a kind of studied fluency, as though he wanted to be Flaubert letting his hair down. But here, as everywhere in *Ravelstein*, there is no straining for effect in writing about a character who is, to all intents and purposes, doing virtually nothing else. 'Crew' refers us to Milton's Satan, and disciples refers us to Satan's rival; the Promised Land of the intellect seems to marry Jerusalem and Athens. Ravelstein, we are told, was 'Homeric', a lover of Plato; a Jew who devoted his life to Athens until he began dying, when he turned back to his forefathers. Chick, though, is not the kind of person who thinks along Jerusalem and Athens lines. If he is anything, in this debate that Bellow has so shrewdly staged, he is literary rather than political. And Bellow, of course, is mindful of what is at stake in such distinctions.

There is, in Ravelstein's view, something childish about the way the literary tend to, as it were, over-personalise things. But Bellow is at pains to indicate what biographers are often at pains to conceal; that writing about someone turns too easily into writing on their behalf. That biographers can be sly when they use their nominal subjects, as novelists use their characters, as a way of saying something they want to say. Ravelstein is Chick's opportunity to voice his misgivings about the literary life, and the literary life story.

But Ravelstein might have argued that there was a danger of self-indulgence in it. Either you continue to live in epiphanies or you shake them off and take up trades and tasks, you adopt rational principles and concern yourself with society and politics. Then the sense of coming from 'elsewhere' vanishes ... In my case Ravelstein's opinion was that distinctiveness of observation had gone much further than it should and was being cultivated for its own strange sake. Mankind had first claim on our attention and I indulged my 'personal metaphysics' too much, he thought.

As 'Ravelstein might have argued' ends up as 'he thought', Bellow conveys just how characters, other people, take on a life of their own in our words; that we are always speaking and writing from other people's point of view, on their behalf. And often speaking in their voices back to them. That we might be full of other people – engaged in endless mutual biography – makes a more private sense of self difficult to account for. For Chick, the privacy of the self is the self: 'My feeling was that you couldn't be known thoroughly unless you found a way to communicate certain "incommunicables" – your private metaphysics.' For Chick's Ravelstein, private metaphysics, 'intimate metaphysics', is the pastime of people intimidated by the publicness of public life. 'A man', Ravelstein believed, 'should be able to hear, and to bear, the worst that could be said of him.' Being assailable is the point and not the problem. You make yourself out of what the world makes of you, and what you can make it make of you. It is purity that is danger. 'He simply believed that a willingness to let the self-esteem structure be attacked and burned to the ground was a measure of your seriousness.' In other words, for Chick's Ravelstein shame is a protection racket; being hated is the acid test of identity.

So, much play is made in this novel by Ravelstein and Chick and Bellow of Chick's New England retreat in the country. In his 'fieldstone house' with its 'old maples and hickory trees' Chick hears very little about what other people think of him. But he has to bear what Ravelstein thinks and that, in a sense, is what Ravelstein is there for. And why, by the same token, Ravelstein has chosen Chick as his biographer. Chick always wants to hear what Ravelstein has to say, and he enjoys hearing it. Ravelstein, who is bored by the country, comes to see Chick out of curiosity; though not curiosity about the country, curiosity about Chick's pleasure in it. 'He had come to the country to see me, and the visit was a concession to my unaccountable taste for remoteness and solitude. Why did I want to bury myself in the woods?' For Ravelstein this is quite literally a kind of death-in-life; and the preoccupation with death, the worry about it, he considers definitively 'bourgeois'. The 'great-souled' live in the knowledge of death, but they don't distract themselves with the terrors or the attractions of it. So for him, 'the drama of the season lacked real interest. Not to be compared to the human drama ... to lose yourself in grasses, leaves, winds, birds, or beasts was an evasion of higher duties.' Thoreau's 'woods' that keep turning up in this book – 'I was not out of the woods' Chick remarks as he begins to recover from his own near-fatal illness towards the end of the book – are for Ravelstein a false solution to the problem of politics, to hearing and bearing what other people say about us; and how this informs what we can hear and say and think about ourselves. To be out of the woods is to be alive, and to be alive is to be in circulation. And once we are around other people our composure is on the line. 'To lose your head', Ravelstein believed, 'was the great-souled thing to do.' It is only with other people that the great temptations of discretion and indiscretion are available.

And yet if *Ravelstein* was more of an allegory than it is – and occasionally it seems like more of an allegory than it is – there would be a simple schema at its heart. There is the solitude of Walden, and Ravelstein dying of Aids. Aids as the worst consequence of a certain kind of free-association; private, intimate metaphysics – burying oneself alive and working out how to get out and how not to – as the worst (or best) consequence of withdrawal. Ravelstein, believing what he believes, and dying in the way he is dying – 'a serious person, not comfortable with himself', as Chick says with Bellow's great ear for the non-sequiturs of character –

becomes for Bellow at once an ultimate form of contemporary nobility, and a test of his fastidiousness as a writer. Ravelstein's 'tact' about his own homosexuality, and his contempt for certain contemporary manners – 'He despised campy homosexuality and took a very low view of "gay pride"' – is matched by Chick's curious blandness about the whole subject. And both Ravelstein and Chick conspire in Bellow's familiar idealisation of a certain kind of woman (what analysts refer to as the wished-for mother of infancy. Chick's young wife Rosamund, for example, is someone with whom 'there was no subject raised which she didn't immediately understand'). In writing about Ravelstein's homosexuality Bellow takes the Greek tragedy approach: the terrible things happen off stage.

We are led to believe that Ravelstein has got up to all sorts of unmentionable things, but the main relationship in the book, with a much younger man called Nikki, is rather more of the loving and caring sort. Nikki is a man of traditionally impressive integrity. And though strongly drawn and, as usual with Bellow, remarkably vivid in his brief appearances, there is something over-stylised about what we are allowed to see of Ravelstein's more passionately fraught life. This is particularly striking given how often Chick refers to, and reiterates, Ravelstein's devotion to the god Eros, to a virtual religion of longing and desire. You get the feeling that Chick (and perhaps Bellow) have Platonised Ravelstein's homosexuality rather more than Ravelstein would always have wished. It's not that there isn't enough fist-fucking in the novel, but that there's a great deal of theorising about the shady concealments people live by, and a too-refined distrust of refinement. A gay bar, you imagine, would be a bar that Chick, at least, would not be keen to go to.

In generational terms Ravelstein's age would have made a certain kind of discretion the order of the day. And yet Bellow's sense of propriety, which is always so accurate, serves another purpose here I think, because Bellow has always written best about the love between men – and especially the hero-worshipping kind – and the love between the generations. And yet it is one of the curious effects of his fiction to make it virtually unthinkable that two men could actually desire each other rather than, or as well as, admire each other or look after each other. In Bellow's fictional world homosexuality is not so much invisible as implausible. And this again is where the putative connection between Ravelstein and Allan Bloom is also a cover-story. Whatever Bloom's attitude was to homosexuality, or indeed to his dying of Aids, Bellow is still making his own decisions as a novelist about Ravelstein. And he keeps reminding us, throughout the novel, that biographies are rather like novels and that this book *Ravelstein* is not a biography, but a story about a man who wants to write one. 'I am bound,' Chick tells us, 'as an honest observer to make plain how Ravelstein operates'; and he is referring both to the inevitable ambiguity of his terms, and to the canny ways this book, also called Ravelstein, operates. What Chick calls Ravelstein's 'endlessly diverting character' is never observed operating sexually, so to speak; what is observed – and Bellow writes with astounding tenderness about Ravelstein's ill body – are the terrible results of Ravelstein's secret (at least to Chick) erotic life. Ravelstein may be diverting, but Chick is diverting us.

The complications that homosexuality throws Ravelstein into – both the character and the book itself – are pertinent because *Ravelstein* is a novel peculiarly troubled by evasiveness. As a fictional character Ravelstein, like many of

Bellow's heroes, is someone forever exercised and en-
ergised by other people's concealments and duplicities.
Bellow's heroes unmask their fellow men and women by
force of character, through a kind of demonic intuition.
They are never programmatically suspicious – they are
never Freudians or Marxists – they have, rather like
novelists, idiosyncratic powers of divination. So Ravelstein
is often getting Chick to face various facts – a keyword in
the novel – about himself and other people; he idealises the
naivety of Eros, the primal intelligence of longing, while
exposing the pernicious naivety of everyday life. Chick, for
example, fails to spot the fascists among his acquaintances,
refuses to see that his wife has put a hex on him, and so on.
Ravelstein is an expert on moral cowardice. 'Why does the
century', he asks, '... underwrite so much destruction?
There is a lameness that comes over all of us when we
consider these facts.' It is part of Ravelstein's 'teaching-
vaudeville' to assail and assault Chick with the plain facts
of the time: the fact, say, that Jews have to live with the
knowledge that quite recently a significant number of
powerful people wanted to wipe them out entirely, and
nearly succeeded. And yet the great glaring facts, the
'world-historical ringside seats' that these Bellow heroes
promote with such amazing eloquence, keep running up
against the centring image of the book, Ravelstein's
increasingly dying body. 'Poor Ravelstein,' Chick says
in an unguarded, awkward moment, 'destroyed by his
reckless sex habits'. We shouldn't evade the big questions,
but we shouldn't use the big questions to evade the other
questions. Bellow has always had a truth-comes-in-blows
sensibility, but in *Ravelstein* there is a new uncertainty
about which blows matter and why. And a strong sense
that there is a difference between talking, however grandly

and wildly and wisely, about recklessness, and living recklessly.

If *Ravelstein* turned out to be his last novel, it would be an extraordinary valediction. But we should hope that it isn't because Bellow is beginning to say new and – to use one of his words – serious things about, among many other things, evasion and recklessness. Evasion is not news, but our evasion of recklessness is.

Steinberg

In Primo Levi's memoir of Auschwitz, *If This is a Man* –
written, he says, not 'to formulate new accusations …
rather, to furnish documentation for a quiet study of certain
aspects of the human mind' – there is an account, that is a
kind of accusation, of a man Levi calls Henri. There are
several character sketches of his fellow inmates in the camp,
but the two pages on Henri are unusually troubled; Levi
tends to know what he thinks of the people he remembers in
this book, but there is something about Henri that makes
him hesitate: 'I know that Henri is living today,' he
concludes; 'I would give much to know his life as a free
man, but I do not want to see him again.' For some reason
Levi clearly didn't want to know the next bit of the story;
what happened to Henri, or perhaps to people like Henri.

Levi's book has the sober lucidity, for which it has been
perhaps too much celebrated, because it has such a clear,
animating intention. Put crudely, it is as though he treats
Auschwitz as a quasi-scientific experiment. As an enquiry
into human nature – in which what people are like in
concentration camps can tell us something about what
people are like – it is assumed that the Holocaust might
teach us something about the roots of morality. For Levi the
experience of being in Auschwitz was above all a learning
experience. Though written as 'an interior liberation', it
documents this particular gruelling piece of contemporary
history to invite moral reflection. It is assumed, in other

Review of Paul Steinberg, *Speak You Also: A Survivor's Reckoning*
(London: Allen Lane, 2000), from the *London Review of Books*

words, that the extremes of human experience can tell us something fundamental, essentially revealing if not necessarily riveting, about human nature. That it is part of human nature to have a human nature, and that therefore everyone's experience is somehow connected, even if at first we can't quite see how (we could all be Nazis and torture people under certain conditions, and so on). Morality (after biology) is a keyword for Levi, who often makes Auschwitz sound like the grotesque laboratory of a mad Darwinian god; and adaptation – another of Levi's keywords – is what is being tested for, the concentration camp becoming a microcosm of how evolution works; of how the human organism, thrown against its will into the harshest of environments, keeps itself going. Morality, in this situation, begins to look like either one of the cleverest or one of the least promising things (or both) that our biology has come up with to help us get on in the world as we find it. So for Levi, it can sometimes seem that what was at stake for him was the whole notion of morality as well as, or instead of, the survival of individuals.

What most interests him, at least in retrospect, is what happened to people's morality – their regard for others and themselves – in Auschwitz. And it was this that made Henri such a problem for him. Because Henri's morality, such as it was, at least in Levi's account, was entirely in the service of his own survival and not the other way round. His life mattered to him more than his (or Levi's) scruples. And this meant that when it came to the crunch, as it frequently did in the camps, his own life mattered more to him than other people's lives. If morality is what we share in order to be able to share anything else, Henri is 'hard and distant, enclosed in armour, the enemy of all'. But Henri is also 'eminently civilised and sane', that is to say, everything that

236

Levi most cherishes and values in life. 'Survival without renunciation of any part of one's own moral world', Levi writes, '... was conceded to very superior individuals'; and Henri was not one of them. Whether or not 'superior individuals' are those who under no circumstances whatsoever sacrifice their personal morality – or, indeed, whether morality at its best is something that should be indifferent to circumstance – is the kind of moot point that Levi is not keen to consider (and if it were true it would presumably also vindicate at least some of the Nazis). But now we have Henri's own version of events – his real name being Paul Steinberg – a book written forty years after the event. A book, in other words, long digested, written with a great deal of hindsight, and indeed foresight; a book all too mindful of the Holocaust industry and so of the genre in which it is written. And a book all too mindful of Primo Levi – who is referred to, one way or another, eleven times in the book – who had, as it were, none of Steinberg's advantages and disadvantages.

If the question now is, why read another Holocaust memoir given we all know the basic story and so can only be further horrified but not surprised, the reassuring answer would be that we read these books for some kind of instruction: though despite Levi's insistence it's not clear what exactly the instruction might be that we seek. Though certainly any other kind of pleasure we might get from such books would be inadmissible (these couldn't really be anybody's favourite books). As knowing about the past, like not knowing about it, often encourages people to repeat it; and the telling of atrocities doesn't seem to diminish their occurrence – they always preach to the converted and incite the rest – we may be better placed now than ever before, as was Steinberg, to wonder what these books are for.

237

Whether, that is to say, they haven't become the fiction of choice for contemporary armchair philosophers, telling us very little about morality and the human condition, and rather more about portentousness and our complicated love of bad news. There has been plenty of great poetry after Auschwitz.

Because imagining the Holocaust, and all the other comparable devastations of contemporary history, is unbearable – imagining, that is to say, what it was like to live hour by hour – we are naturally intrigued by, or even suspicious of those who were able to bear it. Or, in Steinberg's case, able to make something of a success of it. What makes Steinberg's account of 'the after effects of my life in boarding school, as I like to call them' at once so disturbing and so compelling is that he writes of his time in Auschwitz as though he was the hero of a picaresque novel. 'Some times', he writes, with the strange jokiness that characterises the book, 'I think I could have had great expectations for my camp career if only the experiment had lasted longer.' What Steinberg likes to call things in this book, as opposed to what others would like him to call them, is in part what this book is about. And the urgency of recollection in this book is matched by Steinberg's urgent refusal to conform. In the camp, as in the writing of this book, he won't take refuge in the available pieties. 'I must not let the writings of other witnesses affect me,' he writes; but not because he doesn't want to be moved, but because he doesn't want to be recruited. 'I am now certain of what I want to avoid: the museum of horrors, the litany of atrocities. Everything has been said, sometimes too cruelly.' If this acknowledges the proximity of the disgust at human cruelty, and the relishing of it, it is also Steinberg's honourable wish to avoid the gloating in every dirge. How one writes about cruelty without being cruel would seem to be the right question. Memory must always be complicit with what it remembers. The museum and the litany celebrate our losses even as they mourn them.

It is, in a sense, the trickiness of his experience in Auschwitz that seems to intrigue Steinberg. Not the lesson but the luck. 'How can I justify those unbelievable strokes of luck', he asks, knowing just how rhetorical the question is, 'that made me into this fireproof and unsinkable being.' There was, he writes, 'for a lucky few of us, gradual adaptation, the upward climb, and transformation into a different variety of human being, no longer Homo Sapiens but "extermination-camp man"'. *Speak You Also* is nothing if not literary – the title is Celan, the 'happy few' is Stendhal, and great expectations tells its own story, in a way – but it is interestingly haphazard in its ambition and its allusiveness (Levi is always sure, as a writer, about what goes where). That you had to be a new kind of new kind of person to survive in the camps and that a Darwin-Lamarck story comes to mind as an explanation is not strange, given the circumstances (and the times). But Steinberg's question is not, is it immoral to survive if what one does in order to survive is immoral? His question is, is it immoral to be lucky? And one answer would be, it is immoral to be lucky when what you are calling luck is something you yourself have organised. What Steinberg (and the rest of us) like to call luck is sometimes disowned intention masqueraded as coincidence. And sometimes it is luck. Steinberg (like the rest of us) isn't sure quite what he should be taking responsibility for; and he isn't quite sure what he is being held responsible for by Primo Levi. It may be moral luck to find yourself in situations where your moral principles work, but then moral luck is tantamount to never being in a new situation. Or it may be moral luck to come up with the morals you need in any given situation; but then what you like to call your morality is in fact your opportunism. Henri, Levi tells us, was good at 'seducing' people: 'there is no heart so hardened', he writes, 'that Henri cannot breach it if he sets himself to it seriously.' 'Psychologically speaking,' Steinberg writes of himself in Auschwitz, 'I practised all the professions of the circus: lion tamer, tightrope walker, even magician.' He had 'concluded that each one of these monsters (the camp hierarchy) had a flaw, a weakness, which it was up to me to find'. What Levi objects to about Henri is that he uses all the things that Levi most values – 'warmth', 'communication', 'affection', 'he is extremely intelligent, speaks French, German, English and Russian, has an excellent scientific and classical culture' – and yet Levi never feels 'a man to him, but an instrument in his hands'. But interestingly, this makes Levi wonder about Henri, and not about all these virtues and talents that he prizes. As though there must be something suspect about the man that he can use all these precious cultural acquisitions in this way, as if it was all just a survival system. He seems to have acquired a tool kit rather than some essential human goodness. It is, as it were, humanism versus the circus, or rather, Moses against the pragmatists. To read Levi's *If This is a Man* together with Steinberg's *Speak You Also* is in other words a moral and sentimental education for our times.

Steinberg is more interested in the charmed life than the moral life; more interested in what he gets away with than in what he aspires to. For him the road to everywhere is paved with good intentions. So what actually happens fascinates him because his sense of what should happen is so precarious, so uncertain. He was seventeen when he arrived in the camp (Levi was twenty-four), and speculates both interestingly and archly, as is often his way, about whether it was a combination of his youth and his unhappy childhood that had prepared him so well for life in the camp. 'It seems certain', he remarks, 'that a happy stable childhood, protected and full of affection, would have been the worst thing that I could have had.' What, after all, does a good childhood prepare one for? Steinberg's childhood of 'continual displacements and readjustments' meant that he 'would "attend" Auschwitz with invisible resources that vastly increased my chances of survival'. No childhood can prepare one for life because life is not the kind of thing that can be prepared for. And Steinberg's callously ironic references to Auschwitz as a school looks both ways; it refers to what his family life had prepared him for, and it suggests, in rather a different way from Levi, that it was indeed an education of sorts. But what you learnt, if you were lucky, was just how to survive in a concentration camp. 'You had to try to adapt yourself – and be able to make the adjustment. Which right from the outset was impossible for highly structured personalities, men in their forties with social standing, a sense of dignity.' When dignity doesn't work what should we put in its place?

There is none of the 'I am writing this because it must never happen again' righteous sentimentality about Steinberg. If anything, his book is a how-to book for future camp inmates. Indeed what is perhaps unique, and uniquely horrifying, about this book is that its virtue, its human project, even its bizarre generosity, is to try and equip us for life in a concentration camp. 'I heartily recommend to future candidates for deportation', as he likes to call them, in his parody of Levi's university-of-life approach, 'that they enter the medical and paramedical professions, which lead to cushy camp jobs and various perks.' This would be a cynical reason to become a doctor, but it was clearly a lucky choice of profession for those doctors who found themselves in Auschwitz. The unpredictability of life, Steinberg suggests, makes luck the best thing that can ever happen. We have tried to court the world with out integrity; we have been seduced by the romance of morality, but events have overtaken us. If Steinberg in this book is sometimes gleeful about the events he recounts it is partly because he doesn't want our morality to make a mockery of what we can actually do. He doesn't want our principles to make history such a problem for us.

Steinberg's tone in this book is so unsettling not because he relishes these grim truths, but because he didn't want to be fooled by the way his world was. The one thing about himself he wouldn't sacrifice was his talent for improvisation. As he looks back on his fellow survivors to work out what, if anything, they had in common, 'the results of this qualitative analysis are ambiguous'; and this sentence that announces the results is itself a covert parody of an academic approach to such things (what Levi called 'a quiet study of certain aspects of the human mind' is everywhere, wittingly or unwittingly, mocked by Steinberg). Steinberg's findings are that 'the sole common denominator of the survivors seem to me to be an inordinate appetite for life – and the flexibility of a contortionist'. An appetite for life and flexibility are, of course, among our most highly valued secular virtues; but then qualified in the way Steinberg qualifies them makes them look rather different. Clearly nothing in Auschwitz made him feel that life wasn't worth living; or that it was somehow shameful to want to find a way of living in such conditions. This could only be done, though, by not making a necessity of virtue. 'I don't believe in the steadfast hero', he writes, 'who endures every trial with his head held high, the tough guy who never gives in. Not in Auschwitz. If such a man exists, I never met him, and it must be hard for him to sleep with that halo.' It was not their ideals or their principles that got people through, Steinberg thinks, but that 'inordinate' appetite for life that he implies was synonymous with an extreme flexibility. To be a traditional hero in Auschwitz would, Steinberg believes, have been unbearable. Halos are not his thing because most of the traditional virtues that Levi wants in his grave book to preserve were just not an option for the seventeen-year-old Steinberg. He wanted to just survive; and in writing about how he did it he doesn't, by the same token, turn his 'stubborn good luck', his 'frantic desire to survive' into merely another form of inner superiority. He felt himself to be fortunate, but not chosen.

What is most powerful about *Speak You Also* is that Steinberg doesn't know what to make of himself; neither the younger self that he is trying to recollect, nor the much older self who is struggling to write the book. He may not have liked Levi speaking for him and about him; but once he begins to reply, to answer back – and there is an answering of charges as well as an artful defiance in this book, in almost equal measure – Steinberg knows that he is risking something. 'The one thing I am sure of', he writes near the beginning, 'is that writing this will knock me off balance, deprive me of a fragile equilibrium achieved with the utmost care. This imbalance will in turn affect my writing, pushing it either toward greater bluntness or into affectation.' Knowing the pitfalls in such writing may be as much self-knowledge as is available in such situations (and the aim of avoiding bluntness and affectation is surely a shrewd enough critique of much of the so-called witness literature).

But the question of what it is, of what it would mean for a Holocaust memoir to be well-written – and therefore of what is legitimate or appropriate criticism of such literature – is somewhere at the heart of Steinberg's remarkable book; and somehow of a piece with the character of his younger self that he recreates so strikingly in this book. Because there is something stylish about the young Steinberg, as there is about all picaresque heroes, and as there should not be about Holocaust survivors. Steinberg doesn't want to look good, but he does want to look exceptional; exceptional, though, more by luck than judgement. He wants to make it quite clear that he was singled out – and the book is studded with his unusually lucky escapes from (and through) illness, starvation, work and, most miraculously of all, from death just before the liberation of the camps – but that he was nothing special. 'Men in better condition than I went up in smoke'; but he 'made it through, I still don't know how ... Pull – or rather, luck, which has a one track mind.' Equivocations such as this echo throughout the book; but it would be simply glib to assume that he prefers to call it luck rather than his own charisma or cunning just to avoid guilt. One might feel even guiltier, even more insidiously responsible, as the one chosen by chance (if luck has a one-track mind, which track is it?). That one gets by is more appealing to the older Steinberg, than how. That one can feel chosen in the full knowledge that there is nothing or no one in a position to do the choosing; indeed that there can only ever be the wish to be chosen as an absurd cure for the stark contingency of one's life; this is the real message of Steinberg's book. He survived for no particular or obvious reason; he is exemplary because we can learn nothing from his story.

So it is not, as he intimates, exactly a question of pull or luck, because the pull that you have may be as mysterious to you as your luck (the ironist never knows where his knowingness comes from). There must be a sense, Steinberg seems to be saying, in which it is morally better to take responsibility for your actions; but the fact that you can never know either the source or the full consequences of what you do makes the demand for responsibility already punitive. So if Steinberg sometimes sounds wilfully naive in this book – 'If I had known how things would turn out, I would have taken that option' – he also shows us that naivety is the attempt to stage (and thereby seem to master) something that too painfully already exists. If Steinberg has a grievance against Levi – and he is thoroughly temperate and generous in his explicit dealings with him in the book – it is that Levi wouldn't let him off the hook, and it was the hook that mattered too much to Levi. 'He must have been right,' Steinberg writes; 'I probably was that creature obsessed with staying alive … he was a neutral observer, that's how he saw me, and I was surely like that … [with] a gift for inspiring sympathy and pity … Maybe I could have persuaded him to change his verdict by showing him that there were extenuating circumstances.' This is regretful in its way, but it is also morally incisive to describe Auschwitz as 'extenuating circumstances', as though there was something about the camp that Levi couldn't (or wouldn't) see. For Steinberg morality was camouflage, for Levi it was armour.

'The strangest thing about this acquaintance [with Levi]', Steinberg writes, 'that seems to have left such precise traces in his memory is that I do not remember him at all.' As Steinberg is never triumphalist in this book, though he does have the brio to be pleased with himself, he is prepared to give the point a moment's thought. 'Perhaps because I hadn't felt he could be useful to me? Which would confirm his judgement.' There was something about Levi's judgement that was part of Steinberg's noble wish to write his own book. 'Perhaps' is not always a disingenuous word.